Thomas Murphy, Lord Braye

The Position of the Catholic Church in England and Wales

Retrospect and Forecast

Thomas Murphy, Lord Braye

The Position of the Catholic Church in England and Wales
Retrospect and Forecast

ISBN/EAN: 9783744689311

Printed in Europe, USA, Canada, Australia, Japan

Cover: Foto ©Lupo / pixelio.de

More available books at **www.hansebooks.com**

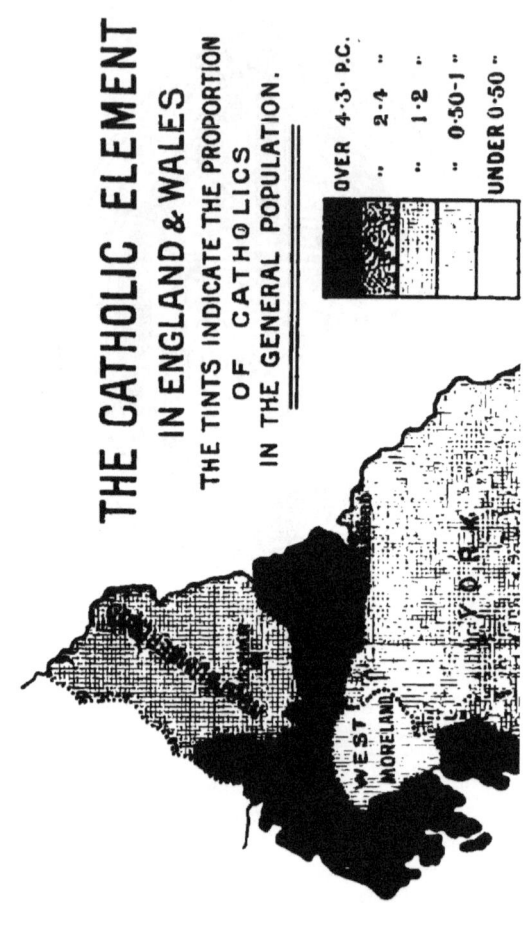

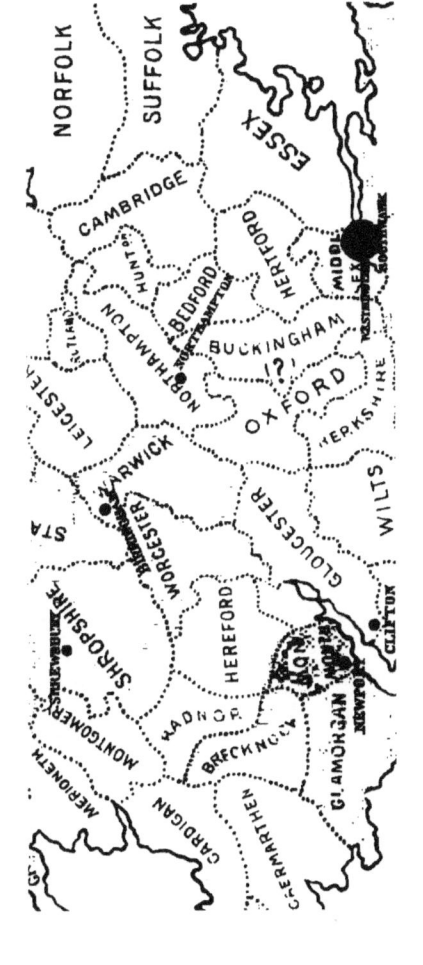

THE POSITION OF THE CATHOLIC CHURCH IN ENGLAND AND WALES DURING THE LAST TWO CENTURIES

RETROSPECT AND FORECAST

EDITED FOR THE XV. CLUB

WITH A PREFACE
BY THE
LORD BRAYE
PRESIDENT OF THE CLUB

LONDON : BURNS & OATES, Limited
NEW YORK : CATHOLIC PUBLICATION SOCIETY CO.
1892
[*All rights reserved*]

ADVERTISEMENT.

IN 1890 the Members of the Fifteen Club offered a prize of fifty guineas for the best Treatise on *The Position of the Catholic Church in England and Wales during the last two Centuries, with special reference to the alleged Progress of the Faith at the present time.* The Club in 1891 awarded the prize to the author signing his paper " One Fold and One Shepherd "—Mr. THOMAS MURPHY of Newcastle in Staffordshire. The Club directed that the Treatise should be published.

PREFACE.

THE future of the Church in England trembles in the balance. Much depends on what the living generation may do to mould the future. The mistake of thinking that England would rapidly return to the Faith—this delusion which prevailed in the middle of the now declining century—is not wholly destroyed; until it is so, there is little hope of real progress.

Such a mistake was a source of great and far-reaching calamity. In the place of building small but numerous mission-houses, men founded churches—nay, cathedrals. Hundreds and hundreds of thousands of pounds were expended on the execution of the designs of clever architects. The building of the walls of Jerusalem was overlooked in the erection of churches made with hands.

The twentieth century will not dawn on a Catholic England. The voice is still sounding which recalls her, but a voice in a desert. In all the sacred pages of Holy Writ there is no expression that brims with greater pain than this—*Vox clamantis in deserto.* We preach the Truth of God, undivided, undefiled—there is none to listen; any or every religion constructed by man, and avowing itself only human, boasting of a fallibility—that is to say, untruth, —any and every such is accepted by the English people.

The fountain and origin of our present disaster is the overabounding hopefulness of our predecessors. Few linger now of that generation; the guiding spirits are gone. They were the pioneers of our way, and we owe them a debt of gratitude simply immeasurable. Their work was noble, but the fruit of it was much marred by the prevailing notion that England was ready to accept the Faith. All men who dare much and do much will make some mistake, even perhaps more palpable than the timid make, who are sheltered by a native obscurity. And their mistake was to overcome the fact of England's vital heresy by buoyant presumption. They imagined anti-Catholicism about to die, and behold it lives, for the punishment of their successors.

Trace to this origin (easy task!) our present disaster. Dioceses overwhelmed with penury or debt, and why? When sees were founded in our country in 1850 parishes were not founded. The missions remained missions, the priests in charge are still missionaries and not parish rectors. Now a bishop with a fixed see in a Catholic country is one institution, and a missionary bishop in a land of the unbelieving is another. England is distinctly a land of the unbelieving, and yet a land whose bishops are not called missionaries and whose priests are. The Holy See, by instituting this combination of ecclesiastical polity, this unusual blending of fixed territorial bishoprics with missionary immunities, thus distinctly traced out the method to be pursued by the laity, for whose benefit these boons were granted. In lieu of building parish churches in remote hamlets, they should have multiplied humble missions to scale of population. The whole centre of charity funds might have been placed in the hands of the Ordinary, who could have dispensed it to the needy missions all over the diocese.

Again, a fixed see must have a seminary—that is, they of that generation thought so. The Council of Trent, distinctly compassionating the poverty of many Christian lands, enacts that dioceses may unite and have one seminary for several.[1] But England was breathlessly re-seeking the Faith. Every bishop must, therefore, under the existing regime, have a seminary; happily many have

---

[1] "But if the churches in any Province labor under so great poverty as that a college cannot be established in certain churches thereof, the Provincial Synod, or the Metropolitan, aided by the two oldest suffragans, shall take care to establish one or more colleges as shall be judged expedient in the metropolitan or in some other more convenient church of the Province, out of the resources of two or more churches in which singly a college cannot conveniently be established, and the youths of the churches shall be educated there. But in churches which have extensive dioceses the bishop *may* have one or more seminaries in the diocese, as to him shall seem expedient," &c., &c.—Council of Trent, sess. xxiii. cap. xviii.

repelled this idea, grown from the soil of error of over-hopefulness before 1850. Who can enumerate the ills flowing from this division of teaching power? Division of teaching power is the weakening of it. In plainest words, talented professors of theology, instead of being able to teach a whole generation, can now but teach a few individuals. Those not in the same diocese are deprived of this instruction. The Divine science of Theology, more precious than any other, is, therefore, difficult of access to the many. If some master of talent in theology comes forward, where are his pupils? Divided in various counties, they cannot be assembled. "Be united, you English Catholics," said His Holiness Pius IX. to the deputation of English youths in 1871. "Remember the motto, 'Union is strength'."[1]

[1] An example of the extraordinary want of power of united action and difficulty of solving the most initial questions as to higher education will be recollected in the uncertainty of any definite scheme of having a Catholic College at Oxford or not. Archbishop (afterwards Cardinal) Manning seems to have been strongly opposed to any idea of Dr. (afterwards Cardinal) Newman establishing any footing at Oxford. Some youths go to the universities with the permission of their bishops, some go without. The following letter (one of many), dated Birmingham, November 2, 1882, will be of interest: "My dear Lord Braye,—You have opened a large field of questions indeed! the difficulty is to select answers or remarks which ought to be made to and upon them. Let me begin abruptly, without considering what should come first or what second. The cardinal question for the moment is the Oxford question. * * * * The Undergraduates and Junior Fellows are sheep without a shepherd. They are sceptics or inquirers, quite open for religious influences. It is a moment for the Catholic Mission in Oxford to seize an opportunity which may never come again. The Jesuits have Oxford men and able men among them. I doubt not that they are doing (as it is) great good there; but I suppose they dread the dislike and suspicion which every forward act of theirs would rouse; but is it not heart-piercing that this opportunity should be lost? The Liberals are sweeping along in triumph, without any Catholic or religious influence to stem them. This is what I feel at the moment, but alas! it is only one out of the various manifestations of what may be called nihilism in the Catholic body and its rulers. They forbid, but they do not direct or create. I should fill many sheets of paper if I continued my exposure of this fact, so I pass on to my second thought. The Holy Father must be put up to this fact and must be made to understand the state of things with us. And I think he ought to do this: he should send here some man of the world, impartial enough to take in two sides of a subject, not a politician or one who would be thought to have anything to do with politics. Such a person should visit (not a 'visitorial' visit) all parts of England, and he should be able to talk English. He should be in England a whole summer. Now, how is the Pope to be persuaded to do this? By some Englishman in position—if

The example of a multiplicity of institutions is soon copied. Colleges dotted the country: again a division and a sub-division of teaching power and a consequent weakening. This separation of our resources has been well pointed out in the Essay before us. The loss of money has been stupendous.[1] Many thousands must have been expended on these splendid buildings—sums which might have supported clergy and missions in almost every town in England and Wales. Debt has fallen like a blight on our impoverished means of evangelising the land.

one or two so much the better. They should talk French and Italian, and remain in Rome some months. This would be the first step. Should anything happen to lead you this way, I should rejoice to have a call.—Most sincerely yours, JOHN H. CARD. NEWMAN." I read the above in Italian to Leo XIII. in 1883, and accompanied by an ecclesiastic in high authority petitioned the Holy Father to graciously consider the suggestions it contained. I also explained that Cardinal Manning was wholly opposed to Catholics going to the two universities, still more to Cardinal Newman or any one else starting a college in either Oxford or Cambridge; that the miserable failure of the impossible scheme of the Kensington Pro-University had brought great calamity on the Catholic body; and, above all, that no alternative mode of education had been propounded by Cardinal Manning. The Pope said he would refer to Cardinal Manning when he came to Rome. Of course nothing more was done in this matter, to the deep regret of Cardinal Newman, who died a few years afterwards (1890). Cardinal Manning, an absolute ruler, whose attitude of non-interference in the vexed question of the higher education of young men was that nihilism above referred to, once wrote to me: "If the laity had gone to Oxford there would have been no laity now". It has been disastrous to the Catholic body in this country that so prominent an ecclesiastic holding this view (with which many may still agree) should never have been able to suggest any compensating method of higher education. He died in 1892 leaving the question unsolved, and no wish or direction, as far as the public are aware, that would help towards a solution. Preaching at the opening of the Jesuit Church in Oxford, after saying he had been informed that Aristotle was no longer an authority at the University, he lamented that Catholics must necessarily exclude themselves from its precincts, and he used this remarkable expression: "We who know its every building and love its every stone, what must this be to us!"

[1] The Bishop of Birmingham (Dr. Ilsley) has set a noble example to the whole body of the Church in our country, by suppressing the boys' school at Oscott—thus cutting off one source of the division of teaching power. The magnificent Tudor buildings and very fine chapel at Oscott must have absorbed a hundred thousand pounds or more, which fifty years ago might have been laid out in missionary work. Gradually the architects themselves may learn that the first object of a missionary Church is not the restoration of Gothic architecture but the restoration of the Faith.

The middle class and the agricultural class, the great bulk of the people, know nothing of the rudiments of the Faith. These sums of money would have supported priests who might, as missionaries, have preached up and down everywhere and throughout the wide deserts of Protestantism.

And this bulk of our people (not having been preached to) still to this hour believe the Church to be a small sect like one of their own. Who is to enlighten them? There is no preacher in countless groups of villages in England and Wales—never has been one since the Reformation.[1] We laity are bound to support not only our bishops, but all the clergy; we, that is to say, the laity of the spirit of the first half of the nineteenth century, have lavished the money on material temples instead, and on many boys' schools, when a few, or even one public school, would have been far better.

The remedy is plain—to labor in season and out of season to reduce in number the channels which drain our means of doing good; to labor for the consolidation of the many seminaries into two or three for the whole province. The same argument applies to boys' schools. To devote the thousands and tens of thousands of pounds thus saved to the payment of the most talented lecturers in theology in these said two or three seminaries; and to found scholarships or exhibitions for our clergy, who are now cruelly harassed with the debts of their forerunners.[2] "Owe no man anything," says St. Paul; and no

---

[1] The *Directory* of 1892 (Burns & Oates) announces that in the county of Radnor there is not one single mission of any kind. It would be a great advantage if Welsh scholarships could be founded, and the clergy by this means could preach in the Welsh language. Without knowing the common language of the people they are trammelled in their missionary efforts. The *Directory* also shows that in England each of the counties of Huntingdon and Rutland has only one priest. In Wales, Montgomeryshire, Brecknockshire, and Cardiganshire likewise have only one priest apiece. Merionethshire is stated to have the services of a priest from April to October in each year.

[2] A splendid opportunity is presenting itself for placing in the hands of our clergy a new means of doing vast good. The study of Greek is being reduced in the centres of liberal education; even at the universities it is rapidly growing less and less. By endowing the study of the Greek Testament in every diocese we could raise the scholarship of our clergy to a high level, and enable them to refute the various Calvinistic heresies with ease and success. Besides which

advice could be more appropriate for future remembrance in every mission of the country, if we may take it in a material sense as applying to debts of money contracted from the love of doing good.

In the eyes of our fellow-countrymen we are one of the many sections and sects which make the Christian religion strange to the unchristian world. "We would believe your religions if there were not so many of them," say the Eastern races to Great Britain's missionaries. But this clamor of sects, differing on essential and primary dogmas, so far from being a proof of their falsehood, is to the British Protestant mind a proof of their activity, and life, and truth. The Catholic Church is numbered among the mass of contradicting factions. Even the educated who come near us and dimly perceive our unity fail to understand the greatness of the Faith. We are counted a small, insignificant, harmless thing.

It is thus with vast objects wrought by Nature or by Art. Who has first beheld the falling floods of the Niagara and not pronounced the sight a lesser than he had hoped to see? But time stretches forth the real immensity of this great ornament of all Earth's waters before the patient and reverent eye. Greater and greater it looms and more beautiful the longer it is seen. So also entering the Basilica on the Vatican Hill ever has the new pilgrim whispered "How small!" But let him walk through the courts of it, lose himself in the spaces of the mansions of it, raise his eyes to scan the spheres of the vaults of it, and then to himself he grows less and less; he seems of no more importance than an insect creeping on the pavement of that temple's unnumbered pavilions. In like manner the Catholic Church overarches the whole of humanity, and essentially one in design, is all variety in the room she affords to the many aspirations of the children of men.

To bring this greatness of Catholicism before the minds of our people, it is necessary to employ missionaries and catechists in the

these endowments or burses would relieve so many priests from penury. Hebrew, Greek, and Latin are the three tongues of the Cross, and to master the three, or even the two latter, is to be equipped with the most splendid panoply a theologian can have as a supplement to his science.

deserts of England. One priest in a country town mission or in a country village mission has to grapple with want of work for six days, overwhelming work on Sundays, and overwhelming debt all days. The Sunday work is most harassing, for the fast before mass tries the constitution severely (in this climate), so that at the evening service when the outside world come (if they come at all they will only come then), he is most fatigued, and the effort of preaching becomes very laborious. How this system would be utterly changed by the simple grouping of missionary centres wherein three or four or five priests, and as many missionary catechists, could live in community! This centre might be a town (any in the desert of heresy); the preachers could drive out to the neighboring lesser towns or villages; the catechists could catechise in a hired room; thousands will imbibe the Faith from catechetical instruction who will not listen to sermons. The labor too of preaching in the morning might thus be saved by aid of catechism, and in such a centre the late mass would only fall to the lot of the same priest monthly instead of weekly. Who can defy the English climate, and who can prevent the morning fast from wearing away and breaking down the health of the preacher? Let the strain be only exceptional and it will do little or no hurt. Add to all this the saving of money by the grouping or centre system thus proposed. One house to keep up instead of many; the diocese thus enriched might found at least an opportunity to the multitude to learn the Faith in every town and in almost every village.

All the want of system which at present prevails arises, as has been shown, not from the fault of any one now living, but from the excess of hope entertained long ago—that is, in other words, the fond presumption that England was coming back all at once to the Church. So dark does the present prospect seem that some have been heard to say that history has not recorded an instance of a nation once having rejected the Faith, ever accepting it again, and why should Great Britain be an exception to the rule! Dark though the prospect be, in every place individuals are ready to renounce heresy if only they knew more of the Faith. By supporting preachers, catechists, and schoolmasters with the money now devoted to stained glass and Gothic magnificence,[1] such opportunity would be afforded. We cannot know from any revelation the best and surest way of propagating the Faith, but surely reason approves of the direct methods. God does not make known the surest details of the work before us; but the general law of missionaries in a missionary country, and no grand temples of stone before the congregations are formed who require them, holds good in England as everywhere else; also the painful experience of all apostleship, that excessive toil is to be expended though little result may appear. In this life there is little to be known, much to be borne, something to be done.

Is England a missionary country, or is it not? If, then, a missionary country, let us set up the missionary apparatus, the method of missionary work, the ways and means of missionary enterprise.

Preaching and catechising need be in no consecrated churches. Have not the greatest Religious Orders sent forth preachers whose pulpits were roadside mounds or desert rocks, whose churches were groves and forests? But even if open-air hymns and sermons cannot be undertaken, there is the humble schoolroom or mission hall. That hero, the first Bishop of Charleston,[2] found no difficulty in the place for his preaching. He went so far as to hire the Protestant meeting-house when he could get no more suitable spot, and expounded the Faith from Calvinistic pulpits. And he was a great and true missionary and is honored in memory as a Father in Christ of countless thousands of Catholics in the New World.

The obstacles to the Great Cause thicken and grow more terrible. The pillars of society seem trembling to their fall.

---

[1] The Roman style of architecture and the Roman vestments are not only far better adapted for a missionary country like ours, but are far cheaper. The dignity, simplicity and uniformity of the Roman ritual, including the plain sacerdotal ornaments, are exceedingly striking, and admit of no representations of saints and sacred subjects, not even of the cross, which in mediæval times were so (as we should say now) roughly and strangely portrayed in Gothic windows and Gothic needlework. The founders of the Brompton Oratory in the classical style have set a noble example to the whole of England in this matter.

[2] See Dr. England's Life in *Catholic Heroes and Heroines of America*. New York, 1885.

The two great crimes which from the earliest ages of Revelation were regarded in their true magnitude as infringements of Divine Law, that is to say, Adultery and Suicide, are wiped away from the modern decalogues of Europe and America. In many countries Divorce may be obtained for a small fee and for no other reason than mutual dislike; in England the conditions are not yet so slender, but the principle of monogamy is gone and the multiplied Divorce Court may wholly efface the tradition of the indissolubility of Marriage. Every other religion is thus utterly opposed to the Catholic Church. She alone teaches that this great sacrament is indissoluble except by death. She teaches monogamy. Again, if a man kills himself the English custom is to declare him insane. If every one who commits suicide is necessarily insane (which seems to be the modern dogma), there is no immorality in the act. But then death is the gate of bliss to every one whether it be self-inflicted or not. There is no mortal sin, no punishment hereafter, the wicked and the just enjoy their rest the instant they die. Cover their coffins with whitest flowers, for they are at peace. That evil motto prevails: *Nil de mortius nisi bonum;* Christianity reads *verum* in place of *bonum*.

Still there is much hope that lingers with us. England clings at least to one Catholic Law, the observation of Sunday.[1] Every seventh day our beloved country makes one grand national Act of Faith in abstaining from servile work. A people who do this still may gather much of true doctrine to themselves. They have not parted with the Faith for ever.

[1] That Sunday *is* a Catholic institution see the very able article in *A Catholic Dictionary*, by Addis & Arnold. Burns & Oates, 1885.

Stanford on Avon,
 April, 1892.

The Catholic Church in England and Wales during the last Two Centuries.

CHAPTER I.

JAMES II. AND THE REVOLUTION.

IN dealing with that period of the history of the Catholic Church in England and Wales which is comprehended within the past two hundred years, it may be well, as a preliminary, to briefly sketch the events which led up to the Revolution of 1688, in order that the position of the Catholics of this country during the latter years of the seventeenth century may be fully understood. The reign of King James II. was one of the briefest in the recorded history of this kingdom, extending as it did only over four years and a few days. Doubtless, the accession of that monarch to the throne gave a ray of hope to the Catholics, who, for a period of one hundred and twenty-seven years, had been subjected to persecution—a persecution of such severity that 319 of their number had been put to death for the mere exercise, or attempted exercise, of their religion. From the virulence with which historians generally have assailed the character of James, it might be imagined he had been guilty of many crimes. It is urged that his actions were unconstitutional. To so argue may be convenient, but assuredly it is not consistent. The Protestant Church had during the reigns of Henry VIII. and Elizabeth been "established" by methods not only unconstitutional but by a system which was responsible for the shedding of blood, for robbery on an extended scale, and for violence. If James had attempted to imitate it in this respect, and none can allege that he did, there were surely historical precedents favorable to such a course. No period of English history has been treated by writers of history at greater length than that of the Revolution. Yet, of these writers, how few to vindicate the action of James, who, as an English monarch, stands out conspicuously as one having many enemies, many critics, but few defenders. It is no part of the duty of a writer, professing to deal with history, to attempt to palliate excesses, or explain away defects. It is generally admitted that in his private character James was blamable; and this is admitted by writers otherwise disposed to defend him. His character, it would appear, was such that he had not sufficient craft to dissemble, and surely that was a point in his favor. His enemies were anxious to distort all they saw or heard, and to attack him from all sides. But there is this striking feature: The quarrel of the opponents of James was not concerning his personal character; that, in the main, appeared to be a matter of indifference. Their quarrel was against James as a Catholic. Had the king been a pronounced supporter of the new religion as established by law, and by methods just alluded to, his defects might have been looked upon as so many kingly vagaries. Whether James, by personally vindicating the principles of liberty of conscience and toleration on the one hand, and the want of dissimulation on the other, tended in the direction of giving to the Catholics another era of persecution, is not now a matter of moment. What James attempted was right in the abstract; but it took nearly two centuries to carry the ideas into effect. When an object sought for is not gained it is no argument to say that the attempt is wrong in itself. If the latter view held good it would follow that all the struggles which this or any other country has undergone for the acquisition of liberty should be set down as so much waste of time because at first unsuccessful. If the action of James was unconstitutional (and the term has come to be accepted), it was because it resulted in failure. The difference between a rebellion and a revolution may be summed up in two words—success or failure. A movement which at first may be termed unconstitutional may, if favored with success, become constitutional: witness as an illustration the revolt of the American colonies. King James II. was not (whatever else may be laid to his charge) a fomenter of civil discord, and to his credit, be it said, the Revolution was a bloodless one. James was not without supporters, and even the Protestant bishops had scruples of conscience when it came to disavowing allegiance to the legitimate ruler of the kingdom, one whom but a short time before they had sworn to uphold. It is said that James wished to subvert the Protestant religion and to make the Catholic Church once more the Church of the nation. There is no actual proof that James had such motives, but even so, such action looked at in the light of history could only be regarded in the light of a piece of regal strategy to which the English people of the sixteenth and seventeenth centuries had not been unaccustomed. The very existence of the new Church was a standing monument, an example, a precedent for this kind of action. But if James had wished to alter the affairs of Church and State by substituting the old for the new, he was well aware there was no opportunity of carrying out any such motive. The "establishment" had become an established fact, and the *ipse dixit* of any writer, no matter how eminent, is not sufficient proof in face of a mass of concrete evidence to the contrary that a thing not attempted was intended to be attempted. In this case, however, the position taken up by many writers is to take the supposed will for an intended deed. What James actually did was to permit some appointments at the Universities to be made. He also attended mass, ostentatiously, it is said, but if so, the latter and generally admitted action goes to prove the transparent sincerity of the man. He would not play the hypocrite, he would exercise his religion openly, and he would permit the harmless Quaker or the persecuted Dissenter to do the same. Had his inclinations so tended he might have enjoyed the Crown undisturbed as his brother had done, in anticipation, perchance, of a deathbed repentance. His candour, however, caused him to feel the full force of the " common struggle against Catholicism ".[1]

CHAPTER II.

WILLIAM III.—1689-1702.[2]

THE third era of persecution for Catholics may be said to have dated from the time when William of Orange and Mary, the

[1] That the Revolution of 1688 was directed against the Catholic Church in England and Wales is generally admitted. Green, in his *Short History of the English People*, writes : " The religious results of the Revolution were hardly less weighty than the political. In the common struggle against Catholicism churchman and non-conformist were strangely at one."

It must not be imagined that even during the reign of James II. the Catholics lived unmolested. From the Historical MS. Commission recently published, XII. Report, Appendix, part vii., we gather the following : " 1688— man named Porter burned by the rabble ". The reason for the burning is added in brutally laconic terms : " He was a Papist ".

[2] " For three hundred years the Catholics were socially and civilly proscribed. They lived—or rather groaned—under all manner of disabilities. It was a crime to profess the Catholic religion, to hear mass, to harbour a priest, to possess beads or medals blessed by the Pope. The legal penalties were fines, confiscation, punishment, torture and death."—Bishop of Salford on " England's Conversion ".

daughter of James II., ascended the throne of England. With the exception of the small Act of Relief of 1778, there was in store for the Catholics a full century of persecution. No time was lost in proceeding to put in force penal laws. In 1687 King James had issued a proclamation "suspending the execution of all penal laws for religious offences, and forbidding the imposition of religious oaths as a test for qualifications". In 1688 the same monarch appended to the previous proclamation one securing for his subjects "Freedom of conscience for ever".

Let the change from this principle be noted. William, by an Act passed in the *first* year of his reign, gave evidence of his interpretation of the terms "liberty" and "toleration". In addition to the oath of supremacy already in existence, he caused the enactment of another still more stringent, in which it was made compulsory for all persons to whom the oath was tendered by a Justice of the Peace to declare that they owned the king as their spiritual Head. The penalty of refusing the oath was that such persons should be punished as "Popish recusants". These "recusants" —that is to say, Catholics—were not allowed to have a horse of above £5 in value; any person might stop a Catholic, and compel him to take that sum for it. As to the clergy: "The prelates and pastors were delivered over to ruffians licensed to hunt them".

Macaulay has painted the "Roman Catholic gentleman" of 1689, or thereabout, cleverly. The picture is scarcely a correct one, even if applied to the time of James II.; but whatever the position of the Catholic landholder under James, a rude change took place during the reign of William III., as we shall see. "The Roman Catholic country gentleman," writes Macaulay, "was neither a fanatic nor a hypocrite. He was a Roman Catholic because his father and grandfather had been so; and he held his hereditary faith sincerely, but with little enthusiasm. . . . The disabilities under which he lay had prevented his mind from expanding to the standard, moderate as that standard was, which the minds of Protestant country gentlemen then ordinarily attained. Excluded, when a boy, from Eton and Westminster; when a youth, from Oxford and Cambridge; when a man, from Parliament; and from the Bench of Justice, he generally vegetated as quietly as the elms of the avenue which led to his ancestral grange. His corn-fields, his dairy, and his cider-press, his greyhounds, his fishing-rod, and his gun, his ale and his tobacco, occupied almost all his thoughts."[1]

But there is abundant evidence that this picture is not in strict accord with historical facts. Reference has been made to the oath of supremacy already in existence, but this was made by William more compulsory in character. In all there were passed by William in his first year of reign three penal measures, including the "Bill of Rights," by which Papists were prevented "for ever" from wearing the Crown of these realms. Concurrently with these statutory measures were passed, or put in force, acts of persecution lesser in degree, but calculated withal to add to the molestation of the Catholics of England. As an instance we learn from records recently published[2] that in 1689 the House of Lords ordered that "no Papist or reputed Papist come near to the House of Parliament or into Westminster Hall".

In 1690 was passed an Act by which Catholics were shut out from the practice of the law and of medicine, or from acting as clerks. On April 11, 1691, from the before-mentioned authority[3] we gather that: "This afternoon two proclamations were published, one for banishing Papists ten miles from London, and tendering the oaths to all disaffected persons". A "disaffected person" at that time, and for a long period subsequently, was interpreted to mean a Catholic. In other words, the effect intended and carried out was that any Protestant magistrate, on mere suspicion of a landholder or person of property being a Catholic, could tender the oaths of allegiance. Refusal to accept the oaths entailed confiscation of property and seizure of goods and chattels. This principle extended through every station, as there is evidence that on October 25, 1692, "Dr. Betts to lose his place in the college [of physicians] if he did not at once take the oath of allegiance".[4] In 1695 the Lords of the Council wrote to the

[1] Macaulay's *History of England from Accession of William III.*
[2] Historical MS. Commission, XII. Report, Appendix, part vii.
[3] *Ibid.*
[4] Oliver's *Collections.*

Dr. Betts was not the only man of distinction who was made to feel the effects of the change. During the stormy time of the Revolution, the Catholics were well represented in the world of letters in the person of John Dryden. Dryden, who was born in the parish of Oldwinckle, Northamptonshire, produced *Annus Mirabilis* and *Alexander's Feast*, the last-named being described as "perhaps the most popular lyric poem in our language". He paraphrased the well-known Catholic Latin hymn, *Veni Creator Spiritus*, but his chief commenda-

Earl of Carlisle "calling for a report of the Papists, and of those who are absent from their homes, and the number of horses and arms seized". In pursuance of this order, the Earl of Carlisle writes to Sir D. Fleming: " I find that you have not arrested any persons except those mentioned in my letter. I think that is not a sufficient execution of the council's order. The principal Papists have been seized in all parts of England, and the same ought to be done in our county." On the 19th March the reply came : " The Papists are so few and inconsiderable, and also the non-jurors in Westmoreland, that they are not dangerous ; moreover, the mob is so averse to them and to Popery, that there would be twenty to one against them ". In addition to these local orders, the Parliament was not slow to continue the work of persecution. In the seventh and eighth years of William's reign (1696) it was enacted that all persons refusing the oaths passed in the first year of his reign (1689) were subject to penalties and forfeitures. In 1697 the Commons petitioned the King for the removal of Papists and non-jurors from London. Two years later an Act was passed empowering the lieutenants of counties " to appoint' and determine such horse and foot soldiers as the estates of Papists may be required to furnish, and to charge the cost of such appointment on their estate ".[1]

In every way, therefore, were the Catholic people ground down. They were first fined for being Catholics, and secondly for so remaining. By the 11 and 12 William III. c. 4, " The private exercise

tion, from a Catholic point of view, lies in his poem, " The Hind and the Panther ". In that great work (book ii.), he defends the Church in a manner not excelled, if ever equalled, by any ecclesiastical writer. There is in it a depth of reasoning, pungency, and argumentative power, such as perhaps never before appeared in any work wherein religious tenets are defended. A prominent writer (Dr. Beard, in his *Biographical Dictionary*) says of Dryden : " He attacked the enemies of the Court with the most bitter satire, and even espoused the Catholic religion, and when deprived of the laureateship by the Revolution, he was left entirely dependent on his literary efforts for support". It has been urged that Dryden changed his religion during the time of James for a pension, and even Dr. Johnson suggests there was an " ugly coincidence " in the matter. This is an apparently malicious statement, because at no time during his life were the Catholics secure from persecution, and the Revolution did not tend to tolerance. That Dryden was consistent is borne out by the pathetic statement, " he died so poor that he was buried by subscription ". Dryden died in 1700, and was interred in Westminster Abbey by the side of Chaucer.

[1] 10 and 11 William III. c. 12.

of the Catholic religion was punished with enormous penalties. By its provision, any person apprehending a Popish bishop, priest, or Jesuit, saying Mass, or exercising any spiritual function, was entitled to a reward of £100.[1]

Pepys in his "correspondence"[2] has a copy of a letter written by him April 12, 1700, from which we extract the following: " I shall here add another bill by which the Parliament, upon what new provocations or considerations I know not, has proceeded to a greater decree of severity against our Roman Catholics than their predecessors have ever done, by condemning all of them, who, being bred up in that profession, do not solemnly renounce it, and take upon them the Protestant religion, at or before the age of eighteen; to forfeit their whole inheritance (be it never so great) and transferring the right thereof *ipso facto* to the next akin; which, they say, do more justify all the King of France does against his Protestant subjects. Another thing, indeed, there is, that looks somewhat a mitigation of our present laws, by repealing so much thereof as subjected to death every Romish priest found among us, by condemning them now to perpetual imprisonment only; but this also that party [the Catholics] take to be much worse than what they were before exposed to, because so seldom found, by the tenderness of our juries exacted from them."[3]

The meaning to be gathered from Pepys' remarks is that whereas the juries might hesitate to condemn a Catholic to death for the mere exercise of his religion, the Catholics anticipated that

---

[1] In Milner's *Letters to a Prebendary* (note 4, letter vii.) there is the following comment on the unjust laws meted out to Catholics by William: "The most severe and unjust amongst those laws was that of 11 and 12 William, by which all Catholics who neglected to take the oaths of allegiance and supremacy, and to protest against their religion as idolatrous according to the declaration of Charles II., were disabled from inheriting the estates of their ancestors, or from making any purchase of land, and by which all Catholic clergymen were subject to perpetual imprisonment, with a reward of £100 for the apprehension of each one of them".

[2] *Pepys' Memoirs and Diary*, edited by Lord Braybrooke. Chandos Library. London: Warne & Co.

[3] Pepys, though "implicated in a charge of Catholicism," was not a Catholic. He was personally connected with King James II., and that was considered a suspicious circumstance. The intolerant spirit exhibited by William and Mary is demonstrated by the statement that " Pepys had been too much personally connected with the king to retain his situation on the accession of William and Mary; and he retired into private life accordingly ".

sentences of perpetual imprisonment might be carried into effect. That this was done for a considerable time after Pepys' death we shall presently show.

Reference has been made to the "Bill of Rights". From its title one would imagine it was a measure for the carrying out of some act of justice. What this bill was we will relate in the candid language of Macaulay: "The Bill of Rights contained some provisions which deserve special mention. The convention had resolved that it was contrary to the interests of the kingdom to be governed by a Papist, but had prescribed no test which could ascertain whether a prince was or was not a Papist. The defect was now supplied. It was enacted that every English sovereign should, in full Parliament, and at the coronation, repeat and subscribe the Declaration against Transubstantiation. It was also enacted that no person who should marry a Papist should be capable of reigning in England, and that, if the sovereign should marry a Papist, the subject should be absolved from allegiance."[1] It has been sought to show for the Prince and Princess of Orange that "they should with pleasure see Roman Catholics as well as Protestant Dissenters relieved in a proper manner from all penal statutes". How the Catholics were "relieved" has been shown; they were legislated for not only during the reign of William but for all time, and by a satiric stroke Protestants were absolved beforehand for a contingency so calamitous in William's opinion as "tolerating" as king or queen one of the ancient faith !

Of the characters of William and Mary compared to that of James II., their friendly historical champion[2] has observed with truth : " In our age enlightened men have pronounced with regret, that on this one point [that of toleration] William appears to disadvantage when compared with his father-in-law ".

However much in the eyes of Protestants William III. may have been regarded in the character of a hero, he was a tyrant in every sense of the word to his Catholic subjects. When his death took place the condition of the Catholics of England was one of deep subjection, and to the modern Catholic student of history the character of William presents not a single redeeming feature.

[1] Macaulay's *History of England*.
[2] Macaulay in his *History*.

CHAPTER III.

QUEEN ANNE—1702-1714.

WHEN at the death of William III. Anne ascended the throne it may have been felt by the Catholics that now surely, under the rule of a woman, a spirit of tolerance would prevail. Or it may have been expected that, having been the objects of penal statutes year by year in the previous reign, there would now be a cessation of such. It would appear as though William had left little to be done by his successor, that he had exhausted all the arts which went to make up everything that was necessary for the punishment of the Catholic body. Though the Catholic memories of the time of Elizabeth were of bloodshed, yet the sanguinary period had closed, and Anne was the first woman who ruled the kingdom in her own right since the time of Elizabeth, a period of nearly one hundred years. If, however, any feeling of hope existed in the minds of the Catholics that their condition would be improved, such feeling was soon rudely dispelled. One of Anne's first Acts was a No-Popery measure, and a new abjuration oath for her Catholic subjects. There was some abatement of the persecution at the commencement of this reign for Dissenters, but not one glimpse of liberty for members of the Catholic religion.

In 1710 was passed an Act for the erection of fifty Protestant churches, and one of the objects sought was "the redressing the inconvenience and growing mischief which result from the increase of Dissenters and Popery".[1] The "Occasional Conformity Act" was passed in 1711. This measure went to enact that all those who had taken the sacrament and test for offices of trust, or the magistracy of corporations, and afterwards frequented any meetings of Dissenters, should be disabled from holding their employments, pay a fine of one hundred pounds, and that no further employment could be held by them till after one whole year's conformity. Doubtless this was specially enacted for the Dissenters, as it cannot be imagined that any Catholic would take the "sacrament" for the purpose of filling a situation. Still it is an excellent picture of the "liberality" of the times, and the insults and degradations heaped alike on Dissenters and Catholics. Several other laws were passed

---

[1] Knight's *Old England*, vol. ii. p. 302.

specially affecting Catholics. In effect these made unlawful the practice of Catholic devotions, the property of Catholics was ordered to be equally divided among their children, so as gradually to impoverish the Catholic aristocracy. "The punishing of Jesuits and other trafficking priests" was a term used in one of the Acts. So rigorous was the execution of these laws that, at the death of Anne, the Catholics of England and Wales numbered, it is said, only 13,000. The spirit of "tolerance" was so far exhibited that a priest could scarcely elude detection, or exercise his ministry in safety. The apostasy of a priest was rewarded by an annuity of £40. Under these circumstances, it could scarcely be expected that the Catholics of that period should entertain other than hostile feelings towards Anne. Neither is it surprising to learn that "Squire Haydock and others, on receiving the news of the death of Queen Anne, and in joyful expectation of the restoration of the royal exiles, 'forthwith indulged in a pig feast to celebrate the event'".[1]

Doubtless "Squire Haydock" represented the feelings of his co-religionists, and we quote the above as an expression of the sentiments which may have prevailed amongst the Catholics generally under the "beneficent" rule of "the good Queen Anne". Her reign was brief, but of sufficient length to add within the space of twelve years still more to the unhappy condition of the Catholics of England and to the extirpation (as far as Acts of Parliament could so tend) of the Catholic Church in this country. But what her predecessors had tried and failed to do Anne also failed in, and the Catholics had at the demise of Anne still another century of proscription before they could emerge from the subjection to which the penal laws were intended to consign them.

CHAPTER IV.

GEORGE I.—1714-1726.

FROM the beginning of Christianity, down to the present moment, the Catholic Church has had to deal with "principalities and powers," and this must ever continue to be one of her distinguishing features. In England the Catholic body have sustained

[1] *The Haydock Papers*, by Jas. Gillow. London: Burns & Oates.

struggles perhaps more severe and lengthened than any other minority in any nation, or at any time; and these struggles were often strangely mixed up with the question of "Protestant succession" to the throne. The succession and the laws bearing thereon were personal matters to William III. and Anne, and during the reign of George I. the question was again to the fore. To maintain the "succession" it was considered requisite to punish Catholics, either by the revival of former acts or by the enactment of new penal measures. A distinguishing feature both of William and Anne was *immediate action* for the suppressing everything favorable to the religious or political aspirations of the Catholics; and this line of conduct George I. was by no means backward in imitating. The Act of Constructive Recusancy, passed in the first year of his reign,[1] was that which, after the accession of the House of Brunswick, the Catholics most sensibly felt. The punishment of recusancy was penal in the extreme, and persons objecting to take the oaths of allegiance and supremacy might be subjected to all the penalties and horrors attendant on recusancy by mere refusal of the oaths when tendered to them.

In order to crush the hopes of the Catholics for the restoration of a monarch of their own religion, it was enacted almost as soon as George I. had ascended the throne, that every Catholic soldier who enlisted without declaring himself a Papist should be punished by court-martial. Other penal sections were contained in the "Act 1, Geo. I. St. c. 2, c. 13," such as that whereby Papists, not taking the oaths required by that particular Act, and omitting to subscribe to the declaration of 30, c. 2, within six months after they came into possession of any lands, or, if let on lease, of the yearly rent reserved to them, were subject to a penalty of £40 and forfeiture. Two-thirds of all penalties to go to the King, and the other to any Protestant who would sue. This was modified by the 3 Geo. I. c. 18, which limited the time for commencing suits to two years. In the same year (1714) was passed an Act for appointing commissioners "to enquire of the estates of certain traitors, and of Popish recusants, and of estates given to superstitious [religious] uses, in order to raise money out of their security for the use of the public".

"The Rebellion of 1715," says a modern Catholic writer, "was not only followed by a rigorous punishment of all Catholics who

---

[1] 1 Geo. I. St. 2, c. 13.

directly took part in it, but it also afforded the commissioners an additional pretext for seizing any Catholic property upon which they could lay their hands."[1]

The Rebellion, if it could be so designated, was a small matter. The Catholic party was strongest in Lancashire, but they were soon cooped up in Preston, and driven to surrender.[2]

Little mercy was shown either by the king or his followers to those suspected of having a desire to place on the throne James Francis, son of James II. At Preston the Earls of Wintoun, Derwentwater, and Nithsdale were taken prisoners. The young Countess of Derwentwater threw herself at George's feet and pleaded hard for her husband's life, but the king was inexorable, and he rudely rejected the appeals for mercy. The Earl of Derwentwater, Viscount Kenmure, and other Catholics were executed on Tower Hill. Every Catholic was an object of suspicion, and it was requisite for literary men of the Catholic religion to exercise the utmost caution. Alexander Pope, the poet, was one who did not escape the attentions of the lynx-eyed minions of the law. The adherence of Pope to the Catholic faith had debarred him when a youth from the advantages shared by his contemporaries, and his education was perforce acquired at such Catholic seminaries as then existed in defiance of the law. In a work lately published we are informed " the religion of the family [Pope's] made their seclusion from the world still more rigid ; the Catholics were then harassed by a legislation which would be condemned by any modern standard as intolerably tyrannical. A Catholic was notoriously a member of a hated minority, but was rigorously excluded from a public career, and from every position of honor and authority. Public exercise of the Catholic religion was forbidden."[3]

---

[1] Payne's *Records of English Catholics of 1715*.

[2] Green's *Short History of the English People*.

[3] *English Men of Letters*, edited by John Morley. *Pope*, by Leslie Stephen.

Knight's *Old England*, vol. ii. p. 346, has the following : " Johnson states, on the authority of Kennett, that on the 2nd Nov., 1713, Dr. Swift came into the coffee-house and had a bow from everybody. Then he instructed a young nobleman that the best poet in England was Mr. Pope (a Papist), who had begun a translation of Homer into English verse." Pope's position as a poet is too well known to call for many remarks here. He was born 1688, the year of the Revolution, and died in 1744. His position as a poet was recognised in his lifetime by the galaxy of literary men who then flourished. In a letter written by the late Thomas Carlyle in 1871 (published after his death), the author of *Sartor*

Priest-hunting was a favorite pastime, as on January 15, 1761, "Father Barrow, a Jesuit, was convicted of recusancy at the Lancaster Sessions, and was declared an outlaw". To use the words of the editor of the *Haydock Papers*, who gives this statement, the proceedings in connection with the hunting of this priest read "like a romance or priest-hunt in the days of Elizabeth". From the same source we condense an account of this particular hunt: "Preston, February 17, 1716. I had a message yesterday that Barrow ye priest sometimes since advise ye of, was selling his goods and making off". Nine days later the same individual had "received the warrant to search Barrow's house, who is both a priest and outlaw'd". On the 8th of March, the "hunter," still in quest of the priest, wrote: "I was yesterday at Westby Hall, but could not find the priest". He then proceeded to make a "very narrow search," with the following result: "Up two pairs of steps in the chapelle, and sounding the walls of the chimney, I found an entrance about 20 inches square, painted as a brick work, which could not have been distinguished by the eye, but striking a spitt into several places I accidentally struck through here, and found a large opening. The convenience of a ladder there fixed, I I went down, and removing some little rubbish, discovered a large quantity of folio books, among which several MSS., a large gilt head of St. Ignatius, some altar linen, and a crucifix."[1]

Resartus wrote of Homer and his translators: "I reckon Pope's still fairly the best English translation, though there are several newer, and one older, not without merit in regard to style or outward garniture, . . . but you will get the *shape* and essential meaning out of Pope as well as another".

Pope, like his predecessor Dryden, was a man of satiric power, and this he employed with great effect in his poems. In a note to Disraeli's *Miscellanies of Literature (Quarrels of Authors)* Pope's humiliating position is thus described: "Pope, in his energetic letter to Lord Hervey, that ' masterpiece of invective, says Warton, which Tyers tells us he kept long back from publishing, at the desire of Queen Caroline, who was fearful her counsellor would become insignificant in the public esteem, and at last in her own, such was the power his genius exercised;—has pointed out one of these causes. It describes himself as a private person under penal laws, and many other disadvantages, not for want of honesty or conscience, yet it is by these alone I have hitherto lived *excluded from all posts of profit or trust*. I can interfere with the views of no man.'"

[1] The severe laws had in some cases the desired effect, viz., the abjuration of the Catholic faith by some of its members. Francis Poole, of Poole Hall, Chester, in his will, dated 1725, evidently forsook his religion. He says: ". . . estate in trust for my half-brother Rowland if he shall at my decease profess the

On the 10th of March the search was continued, and after a "thorough search," there was found " priests' vests, some altar and household linnen, and a large picture of ye Virgin Mary ". The goods were seized, even a great quantity of hay " sold by public auction ". But it appears there were occasionally difficulties in the way, as in the case of Gartside's goods, when " Mr. Mosman and self were sworn appraisers, but nobody buying, I was forct to bid by another hand, and take the goods in my possession, so that the act was comply'd with ".

No better instance than the above could be afforded of the cruelty of the operation of the recusancy and other acts, and it may also be regarded as an authentic record of the position of Catholics generally at that time.

A Protestant writer [1] treating of the reign of George I. remarks in his work : " Popular outbreaks against Dissenters sometimes occurred, but so far as law and government were concerned full liberty of worship was allowed except to Roman Catholics ".

The attitude of the prelates of the Established Church was one exhibiting a great want of Christian charity. These men lent themselves as agents and propagators of the anti-Catholic spirit. Even the clergy acted as spies. The following quotation will prove the correctness of the assertion, and it is given on the authority of the Dean of Winchester in a work published so recently as 1890. This work states : " Bishop Trelawney, translated hither by Queen Anne in 1707, was one of the famous seven bishops to petition King James II. against the Declaration of Indulgence. Years after Trelawney came to Wolvesley we find that his spirit was greatly disturbed by the audacity of the Romanists in the city, who boldly attended the worship of their church, and had even shown themselves in the persons of their priests. The bishop therefore called upon the mayor to put in force the severe laws against the Romanists. We have a full account of it all in Bishop Trelawney's letter to Archbishop Wake dated April 28, 1720 : ' Being informed that mass was said in the

Protestant religion according to the Church of England as now by law established, or shall, in six lunary months, conform thereto, and qualify himself in such manner as by the law and statutes of the realm persons professing the Roman Catholic religion are obliged to conform, in order to take lands by descent or devise ".—Payne's *Records of English Catholics*, p. 7.

[1] *History of Religion in England*, by J. Houghton, D.D. (1881).

city and some priests were very busy and too successful in their perversions, I ordered my register to acquaint my clergy to be on their guard, and to desire the mayor to observe the frequenters of it, and to tender the oath to all suspected persons '."[1]

This system of persecution was productive of one effect—that of impoverishing the Catholic body. Such as were possessed of this world's goods did not hesitate to succour their less fortunate brethren. We find in a record of the time that John Weston of Sutton Place, Surrey, in his will, 22nd November, 1724, adds thereto: "Whereas the miserable condition of the poor Catholics of England is very deplorable, in consideration thereof I bequeath to the poorest and most needy of them £250, to be divided amongst 500 poor, which is 10s. a-piece".[2]

Many other instances of the results of despotism could be given, but in the above will be found the general tenor of the system under which Catholics labored during the twelve years of the reign of George I.

CHAPTER V.

GEORGE II.—1727-1760.

THE learned Doctor Challoner, who for half-a-century was destined to work on the English mission, left Douai on August 18, 1730. This was three years from the time of the accession of George II., and a time also when the laws against the Catholics were a great restraint on Catholic preaching. In the public chapels few sermons were allowed, but some zealous missionaries preached in the rooms of individuals or in rooms specially hired for the purpose, and even in public-houses. A room in the Ship alehouse,[3] near Lincoln's Inn Fields, was frequently used in this manner, and in such places Dr. Challoner was often heard.

During the earlier portions of the ministrations of that ecclesiastic, the Catholic body scarcely dared erect a chapel, however

---

[1] From *Historic Towns*, edited by Freeman and Hunt: "Winchester," by G. W. Kitchin, Dean of Winchester. London: Longmans & Green, 1890.

[2] Payne's *Records of English Catholics of* 1715. London: Burns & Oates, 1889.

[3] See account of the Gordon Riots and the "Ship Inn," p. 36.

humble, wherein to worship. Only in the halls of the Catholic gentry (and not in every case there) was it possible to celebrate the holy sacrifice. Bishop Challoner had to avail himself of the accommodation afforded in friendly public-houses, and for preaching a cockpit was used. Bishop Milner had often seen him and heard him on these occasions, and used to relate sermons which were delivered in a cockpit hired for the purpose.

About this time several persons were indicted by the "Protestant Carpenter" for assisting at Mass. This "carpenter" was of the informer species, and gained a livelihood by detecting Catholics in the exercise of their religion. For such a class there was abundant work. But there were others of a class higher in the social scale than the carpenter, as Richard Smallbroke, Bishop of Lichfield, in his charge 1735-6, spoke of the "extraordinary efforts to spread Popery".[1]

It would be well here perhaps to sketch the condition of England in the year 1742. The picture we give is that of a Protestant writer, and may be accepted as an unbiased statement as to the position of the people generally after one hundred and sixty years of Protestant rule, and a corresponding period of Catholic persecution. "A shrewd if prejudiced observer" (writes Green in his *Short History*) "brands the English clergy of the day as the 'most remiss of their labours in private, and the least severe in their lives'. There was a revolt against religion and against churches in both the extremes of English society. Of the prominent statesmen of the time, the greater part were unbelievers in any form of Christianity, and distinguished for the grossness of their lives. The poor were ignorant and brutal. Not a new parish had been created. Schools there were none, save the grammar school of Edward and Elizabeth. 'We saw but one Bible in the parish of Cheddar,' said Hannah More at a far later time, 'and that was used to prop a flower-pot'. Within the towns things were worse. There was no effective police, and in great outbreaks the mob of London or Birmingham burnt houses, flung open prisons, and sacked and pillaged at their will. In the streets of London at one time gin shops invited every passer-by to get drunk for a penny, or dead drunk for two pence."

As an indication of the spirit of the times, it may be here re-

---

[1] *Diocesan History of Lichfield.* London: Society for Promoting Christian Knowledge.

marked that on Feb. 27, 1744, John Wesley wrote in his *Journal*: " Mon., 27, was the day I had appointed to go out of town; but understanding a Proclamation was just published, requiring all Papists to go out of London, before the Friday following, I was determined to stay another week, that I might cut off all reason of reproach ". On March 5, following, Wesley wrote an address to the King, headed " The Humble Address of the Societies in England and Wales, in derision called Methodists ". In that address Wesley protested that his followers were " still traduced as inclined to Popery ". He further protested that, whilst declaring " our most dutiful regards to your sacred Majesty . . . we detest and abhor the fundamental doctrines of the Church of Rome, and are steadily attached to your Majesty's royal person and illustrious house". Thus were Catholics in a cruelly isolated position ; and their loyalty and religion were equally matters of suspicion.

Occasion has been taken to associate the Catholic name with the Rebellion. Whether or not the Catholics were promoters or abettors of the Rebellion is not a matter of moment, but it is noteworthy that a popular writer of our own time, in a history[1] regarded as a standard work, says : " Catholics and Tories abounded in Lancashire, but only a single squire took up arms ". During this time it was necessary for the Catholics to use the utmost care on making their bequests. Walter, Lord Aston, by a codicil to his will, leaves "£100 for prayers for his soul—viz., £50 to the two bishops in London, Mr. White and Mr. Challence ". In a note to this, quoted from the *Douai Diary*, p. 85, *White* was an *alias* of Bishop *Benjamin Petre*, who at the date of Lord Aston's will was Vicar-Apostolic of the London District, Bishop Challoner [*Challence*] being also then his coadjutor.[2] A proclamation was issued 6th December, 1745,[3] for putting the laws into execution against Jesuits and Popish priests, and promising a

---

[1] Green's *Short History of the English People*.

[2] Payne's *Records of the English Catholics of 1715*.

[3] It is memorable that this very year, 1745—the year of Culloden, witnessed the first official permission of Catholic worship in the British Isles, not, however, in Great Britain, but in Dublin. The Duke of Devonshire, the Viceroy, persecuted the Catholics with great severity in 1743 and 1744, but the following year their calamities moved the Government to compassion, and on March 17 (St. Patrick's Day) all the chapels in Dublin were opened and have remained open ever since.—See Myles O'Reilly's *Memorials*, p. 375. Burns & Oates, 1868.

reward for their apprehension within London. A project was also set on foot to make the Catholics pay two-thirds of their income to the support of the Government. In 1745 James Cosen, son of a former secretary to the Committee for Forfeited Estates, published a list of persons who refused to take the oaths of King George. The list also contained the names of those who complied with an Act of Parliament 1 Geo. c. 55, intituled, "An Act to oblige Papists to Register their Real Estates ".[1]

Before the year 1752 Great Britain adhered to the "old style" of calculating the calendar. Every European country, with the exception of England, Russia, and Sweden, had adopted the "Gregorian" method formulated by Gregory XIII. in 1583. By the middle of the eighteenth century, the error of the old style had increased eleven days. A bill was passed which ordered the year to commence on January 1 instead of March 25, causing eleven days in September, 1752, to be nominally suppressed, and introducing the Gregorian method of calculating the calendar. Strange as it may appear, the measure was regarded by many as a Popish innovation which defrauded them of eleven days !

It is only fair to add that Bishop Walmesley, a profound mathematician (subsequently appointed coadjutor of the Western District), was consulted by the Government on the alteration of the calendar.[2]

[1] Payne's *English Catholic Non-Jurors of* 1715.
[2] Charles Walmesley, O.S.B., Bishop of Rama, was consecrated 21st Dec., 1756; died 25th Nov., 1797, æt. 76.

Notwithstanding the cruel disadvantages under which the Catholics labored, they were not destitute of eminent men. Of these, two deserve honourable mention; viz., Dr. Hawarden, Professor of Theology at Douay College, and Bishop Walmesley. Dr. Hawarden wrote in defence of the Trinity, then attacked by Dr. Samuel Clarke. He silenced his opponent by a single question ; and Clarke was compelled to acknowledge himself vanquished. The genius of Bishop Walmesley was of a different kind. As before stated, he was one of the mathematicians of his time ; and at the age of twenty-five his scientific writings had already won for him the honours of several foreign academies. He was consulted by the English Government on the alteration of the calendar ; and in 1756 become coadjutor of the Western District. But he was a man of piety even more than he was a man of talent, and is said to have abandoned his favorite pursuits from the circumstance of their having once caused him a distraction whilst saying Mass. D'Alembert expressed his regret at the loss thus sustained by science ; but the bishop never wavered in his generous resolution, though to the last his countenance would brighten if the subject of mathematics was mentioned in his presence.

About this time the marriage laws were a source of great annoyance to the Catholics, and so remained until 1837. In 1753 Dr. Challoner exerted himself to the utmost of his power to prevent so much of the Marriage Act, then brought into Parliament, from being enacted as required the celebration of marriage in Protestant churches. In these exertions also he was assisted by the Duke of Norfolk, but they were fruitless: he obtained, however, the most explicit assurances, from those whose declarations on the subject were of authority, that the attendance of Catholics in Protestant churches on these occasions was considered by Government and the public, not as an act of religious conformity, or as a communication with Protestants in sacred worship, but as "a ceremony prescribed by the law of the land for the civil legality of the marriage". The extreme necessity of the case induced Dr. Challoner and the other vicars-apostolic to think such marriages might be tolerated; but they enjoined the faithful not to join externally or internally in the prayers of the Protestant minister; to avoid, when it could be done, kneeling when the minister pronounced the nuptial benediction; and previously to the marriage in the Protestant church, to be married by the priest.

The attitude of the heads of the Church of England towards the Catholics was by no means altered. A Nonconformist writer, dealing of the period, says: "Some of the Church of England hated Rome, and they hated Geneva. Papists in their estimation were idolaters. Neither had the condition of the people altered in another important aspect. The moral character of the clergy was no better than the material surroundings. Drunkenness was not unknown even in the House of God. Shameful immoralities of

---

Another eminent man of the period was Alban Butler, the author of the *Lives of the Saints*, and a man of extraordinary and varied learning, was President of St. Omer's College at the close of the reign of George II. The *Lives of the Saints* is an exhaustive work, the learning of which, though certainly not the style, rivals the contemporary work of Gibbon. Gibbon became a Catholic when only fifteen, but soon afterwards apostatized. His genius, thus corrupted, has done great harm to the cause of Christianity in this country.

We have previously mentioned the name of Bishop Challoner. It may be of interest to many Catholics to note that Challoner was converted to the faith by the celebrated Gother; and as the author of the *Meditations*, the *Think Well On't*, the *Lives of the Missionary Priests*, and the *Garden of the Soul*, his name is deservedly held in veneration by every English Catholic.[1]

[1] From *History of England for Family Use*.

other kinds were on sufficient grounds attributed to clerical incumbents" (p. 44). In the same work, p. 48, we read: " Hence it appears that the National Church, with all its resources, had failed to purify the atmosphere of the country ".[1]

To sum up, it may be said of the thirty-three years of the reign of George II. that the position of the Catholics was in no better a condition at his death than when he ascended the throne.

CHAPTER VI.

GEORGE III.—1760-1820.[2]

KING GEORGE III. in the first year of his reign signalised his accession to office by passing at least one law which by some has been characterised as a penal measure—the prohibition of Catholics from serving in the militia. The year following, however, a "remedy" was discovered, it being enacted by the 2 Geo. III. c. 20 that every man enrolled in the militia should take an oath of allegiance and conformity, and one section contained the words, "and I do swear that I am a Protestant". Officers in higher grades were compelled to take a similar oath.[3]

Another penal measure passed early in the reign of George III. was that which subjected Papists over eighteen years of age *refusing* or *neglecting* to take the oaths (which as Catholics it was impossible for them to take) to a double assessment of the land tax.[4] The Catholics were still an obscure class. In Exeter, from their poverty and small number, they were obliged to be satisfied with the occasional attendance of a clergyman, but about 1762 the Jesuits undertook to provide a regular incumbent. For many years Divine Service was performed in a poor room in Mr. Flashman's house, called at that time King George Tavern. In

---

[1] Stoughton's *History of Religion in England*, vol. vi.

[2] " Even the fathers of men now living remember the time when the only safe way for a Catholic to retain his estates was by legally conveying them to a Protestant, and when a Catholic could be compelled by any stranger on the road to give up his horse for a five-pound note."—*England's Conversion*, by the Bishop of Salford, 1890.

[3] See Madden's *Penal Laws against Roman Catholics*. Dublin: Richardson, 1847.

[4] 4 Geo. III. c. 3.

1775 a lease was taken of the " Capital Mansion commonly called or known by the name of St. Nicholas," and a large upper room was easily formed into a chapel. For many years the faithful of Plymouth were in a worse condition than even their brethren in Exeter. Their chapel was merely a garret at Coxside. From 1765 to 1770 the priests suffered much persecution from informers. There was one Paine who endeavoured to traffic in the penal laws by " earning " the fine of £100 upon the conviction of each priest when apprehended. There is reason to believe that many of those wretches were set on by certain principal persons, but it is equally true they were discouraged as much as possible by members of the Government and the courts of judicature. These proceedings were condemned by the Bishop of London, the Lord Mayor, and other influential personages, and it was difficult to find juries to return bills. After the " offenders " were found warrants were obtained and the indicted persons were taken into custody. Dr. Challoner and others were indicted, but from the difficulty of establishing the facts he and others escaped punishment.

Mr. Payne in his work [1] has the following, quoted from the *Universal Museum* for March, 1767 : " Another Mass House was discovered in Hog Lane, near the Seven Dials. . . . John Baptist Malony, a Papist priest, was taken up for exercising his functions in Kent Street contrary to law. . . . He was convicted at Croydon, August 23, and sentenced to perpetual imprisonment."

The Rev. James Webb was tried for being a priest in the Court of King's Bench, 25th June, 1768.[2]

In 1770 " Sir William Stanley of Horton, Bart., was indicted for refusing to part with his four coach-horses to a Church dignitary, who had tendered him a £20 note ; but was acquitted on the ground of its not being a legal tender ".[3]

The first indulgence shown to Catholics was in 1778. A petition framed by Edmund Burke was presented to the king. It was signed by the Duke of Norfolk, the Earl of Shrewsbury, and others. The result of this was that a Bill was brought into Parliament by Sir George Savile for the repeal of certain penalties and disabilities, including the punishment of officiating priests as

---

[1] *Old English Catholic Missions.*
[2] Butler's Biographical Account of Dr. Challoner. *Catholic Spectator*, 1824.
[3] Oliver's *Collections*, p. 15.

felons or traitors; the forfeiture to which Catholic heirs educated abroad had been subjected in their property; the power given to a son or near relation, being a Protestant, to take possession of a father's or other relative's estate, and the depriving them of the power of acquiring landed property by purchase. The motion was received with universal approbation, and the Bill was passed into law without opposition.

Mild as was this measure of relief, it led up to the events chronicled in the next chapter. We have already given instances of the hostile attitude of the religious teachers of the people in connection with the position of the Catholic body. This hostility was by no means lessened so late as the year 1781, and we give this on the authority of a Protestant writer, whose account may be looked upon as an accurate description of the feeling prevailing at that period.

"There was one defect," says Canon Molesworth,[1] "which at this time characterised almost all the communions into which the religious world was divided: whether Methodists or Nonconformists of other denominations, High Churchmen or Low Churchmen, orthodox or evangelical, they were all ready to combine for the purpose of perpetuating the scandalous disabilities which had been laid on the Roman Catholics. Even the most ardent advocates of civil and religious liberty, the moment that the Catholic Church was in question seemed to cast away their principles, and to become the advocates of the most abominable tyranny."

CHAPTER VII.

THE GORDON RIOTS—1780.

THE British constitution, as the term is understood, and of which the English citizen is so proud, is a thing that has been built up by degrees—a thing of gradual growth. Our freedom to-day as a people (and we speak now of the people generally), whether affecting religion, politics, or the possession of constitutional rights, has not been attained without severe struggles, which led even to bloodshed. At times the people have risen, and justly too, in revolt against the treatment meted out to them by their rulers. On the

[1] *History of the Church of England from* 1660.

other hand, it has been occasionally necessary to protect the people against their own acts of folly. Constitutionalism is equally concerned in the maintenance of order as it is in the preservation of the rights of the people. Not always have the English people enjoyed that freedom and liberty of conscience which is a distinguishing feature of the England of to-day, and the possession of which has made her a nation to be envied among the peoples of the earth. England is the refuge of the exile, from the discrowned monarch to the Russian socialist or the persecuted Jew. Within the shores of free England neither proscription nor conscription prevail, and it is no exaggeration of speech to say that the hope and prayer of all good citizens is that that spirit may ever prevail.

But of the past as much cannot be said. And if there is one period of which more than other the average Englishman looks back to with shame it is to that period of Catholic persecution known as the Gordon Riots of 1780. It has been dealt with by historians, orators, and statesmen, and to the credit of Englishmen they have not through their men of learning and culture hesitated to express in language most forcible their abhorrence of the attitude of the common people towards their fellow-Catholics during that short period of rapine, plunder, persecution, and bloodshed. The following is the expression of a man eminent as an orator, a man who in his day was one of the most brilliant members of the House of Commons—Edmund Burke. " In the year 1780 there were found in this nation men deluded enough (for I give the whole to their delusion) on pretences of zeal and piety, without any sort of provocation whatsoever, real or pretended, to make a desperate attempt which would have consumed all the glory and power of this country in the flames of London, and buried all law, order, and religion under the ruins of the metropolis of the Protestant world."[1]

The man who gave utterance to these words was one who spoke with full knowledge of the circumstances, and was witness to the scenes of violence.

Sixty-seven years later another man, who, if not equally gifted with language, has achieved greatness as one of England's writers, said of that period (1780), when addressing the House of Commons on the Education Question: " I speak of the No-Popery riots; I do not know that in all history there is a stronger proof of

---

[1] Edmund Burke, Speech to the Electors of Bristol.

the proposition that the ignorance of the common people makes the property, the limbs, the lives of all classes insecure. Without the shadow of a grievance, at the summons of a madman, a hundred thousand people rose in insurrection. During a whole week there is anarchy in the greatest and wealthiest of European cities."[1] The agitation which culminated in the Gordon riots was commenced in the month of January, 1780. A deputation calling themselves the " Protestant Association " waited on Lord North requesting him to present a petition to Parliament in favor of the repeal of the laws recently passed in favor of the Catholics. During the subsequent Parliament Lord George Gordon, a member of the House of Commons, took frequent occasion to interrupt the proceedings of that body in a form which in our time would be called "obstructive". The mania which seemed to possess the young Scottish lord was that of the "dangers of Popery". As a consequence of his inflammatory harangues the mob on the 2nd of June proceeded to the House of Commons to enforce if possible the presentation of their petition. The debate on Lord George Gordon's motion was defeated by 192 to 6. This seemed to madden Gordon and to incense the mob.

The House of Commons was terrified, and for a while the authorities seemed powerless. The mob proceeded at once to give vent to their feelings by acts of violence. They destroyed the Catholic Chapel in Duke Street[2] belonging to the Bavarian ambassador, and the Bavarian Chapel in Warwick Street. They attacked the Bank of England, which was, however, protected by soldiers. The prisons were forced open, the toll gates attacked and plundered of the money to be found. As the night advanced the glare of conflagrations filled the sky. Dr. Johnson, who was an eye-witness, writes: " The sight was dreadful," and it was

[1] Macaulay, Speech on Education, 1847.

[2] *The Lamp* (October 10, 1857) contained the following interesting account of the removal of the sacred vessels from this chapel: " There lately died at Hampstead Mrs. Ann Roberts, aged ninety-three years. It was Mrs. Roberts that took the sacred plate from the sacristy of Duke Street Chapel, Lincoln's Inn Fields, when Lord George Gordon's rioters were trying to burn down the chapel. She took them to the priest that was in hiding at the Ship tavern, at the corner of Turnstile, Gate Street, Holborn, and as he was fasting he said mass in thanksgiving for the recovery of the Blessed Sacrament and the sacred vessels, in a room on the first floor, upon an altar-stone laid on a table, with one cloth doubled three times, two candles, and a small missal which the priest took out of his pocket, and Mrs. Roberts served the mass."

computed that thirty-six fires were blazing at one time. That London was not destroyed was due to Providence. "The night was perfectly calm and serene," says Lord Mahon, "the slightest wind might have stirred the flames and reduced a great part of London to ashes. The principal scene of that night of horror was at Holborn. There," says our authority,[1] "the mob had burst open and set on fire the warehouse of Mr. Langdale, a Roman Catholic and a distiller. His large stores of spirits were poured forth in lavish profusion, and taken up by pailfuls; the kennel ran gin, and men, women, and children were seen upon their knees eagerly sucking up the liquor as it flowed. Many of these poor, deluded wretches were stirred to the most frantic fury; many more sank down in helpless stupefaction, and too drunk to move perished in the flames which had been kindled by themselves." Disgraceful inactivity prevailed among the magistracy and members of the Government. Ten thousand of the military were at hand, but there was no one with sufficient firmness to put them in action. Whilst the mob were sacking London, there was quibbling in high quarters as to whether it would be legal to fire before the Riot Act had been publicly read. "The King was the first to show energy and determination. It was from him rather than any of his subjects that came the measures of protection. Till then such had been the craven spirit of some men in authority that, according to the Duke of Grafton, the Secretary of State's servants had worn in their hats, as a passport, the cockades of the rioters."[2]

Wedderburn, the attorney-general, grasped the situation, and at a council called by the King said that, in his judgment: "Neither the delay of an hour nor any such formality is by law required when the mob are engaged in a felony, as setting fire to a dwelling-house, and cannot be restrained by other means".

The King concurred in this, and said: "There shall be at all events one magistrate in the kingdom who will do his duty". The military were called out, and the mob were soon subdued. In one case the rioters had taken possession of Blackfriars Bridge. At that place several were killed by the musketry, while others were thrown, or in their panic threw themselves, over the parapet into the Thames.

From another Protestant writer is taken the following unpre-

---

[1] Lord Mahon's *History of England*.
[2] *History of England*, vol. vii.

judiced account: "Lord Mansfield was one of those tolerant men who showed liberality both to Catholics and others. A bill had been introduced in the early part of the reign of William and Mary that contained clauses condemning a Roman Catholic to fine and imprisonment for life if he said Mass, and that disqualified a Papist from becoming a proprietor of land, either by inheritance or purchase. A bill being introduced for the repeal of these odious provisions, Lord Mansfield gave it his hearty support. This caused a spirit of bigotry. Out of this came the fanatical spirit of which Lord George Gordon was the head. Catholics were declared followers of anti-Christ. The mob attacked every one suspected of sympathy with them. The peers were ill-treated, and even the Protestant Archbishop of York and the Bishop of Lincoln, falsely accused of leaning to Popery, were with great difficulty rescued from the mob. Of the rioters 210 were killed and 248 wounded."[1]

The venerable Dr. Challoner seemed an especial object of the hatred of the rabble, and his name was particularly obnoxious.[2]

A party of the rioters were proceeding to Bishop Challoner's house, in Gloucester Square, about eleven o'clock at night. The Bishop had to fly for his life. "Many had sworn to roast him alive. Castle Street, Holborn, where the humble dwelling was situated, swarmed that night with the rioters, who were vainly seeking for his house. The number had been accurately supplied them, but either from drunkenness or the mercy of God's protecting Providence, they failed to discern it. We may faintly guess the horrors endured by this aged prelate when the frequent shouts for the Popish bishop to come forth assailed his ears. He remained during that long and agonizing interval upon his knees, praying with his accustomed fervor to his Heavenly Master to give him that fortitude and resignation which might sustain him in his

---

[1] In Madden's *Penal Laws* (p. 246) there is the following statement: "Five hundred dead and wounded lay next morning in the streets, and the yells of 'No Popery' had ceased to be heard in the late frightful scenes of pillage, bloodshed and tumult in the capital of the 'most civilised country of the world'".

[2] Dr. Challoner died 12th January, 1781, and though full of years his death was no doubt hastened by the horrors of the terrible night of 2nd June. He was buried in the Parish Church of Milton, Berkshire, and the incumbent entered his death in the parish register in the following terms: "Anno Domini, 1781, January 22. Buried the Reverend Richard Challoner, a Popish priest and titular Bishop of London and Salisbury, a very pious and good man, of great learning and extensive abilities."

threatened martyrdom. If those aged eyes shed tears they were not for his own calamities, but for those of his flock who, like the early Christians, were exposed to the wild beasts."[1]

" The insurrection extended all over England, and one Catholic chapel was burned at Bath and another at Hull, and Catholics were everywhere threatened with destruction."[2] Another authority[3] says: " In June, 1780, the rioters attacked and burnt Bishop Walmesley's house, in Belltree Lane, Bath ".

Many more instances might be cited from the records of local historians of the havoc wrought, and the reign of terror under which Catholics existed during that unhappy week, but one more quotation shall suffice. Not only were the Catholics of London and the large towns attacked, but the contagion spread even to the most remote parts. At that time the Catholics were presuming to erect humble chapels in various parts of the country, and in the year 1780 the Catholics of North Staffordshire proceeded to build a small chapel at Cobridge, at that time a remote hamlet. The chapel was to serve as a place of worship for Catholics for many miles in all directions. It is not surprising to learn from a county historian that: " The walls of this chapel had just been raised above the ground when the Protestant riots in London, with which the name of Lord George Gordon is associated, took place, and the alarmed Catholics of Cobridge suspended their building for several months ".[4]

And so we conclude this necessarily brief and condensed account of a time of tumult and danger to the Catholics and to the country at large. And of it the sentiment of every well-meaning citizen will at this time of peace and religious equality find a re-echo : " I do not wish to go over the horrid scene that was acted. Would to God that it could be expunged for ever from the annals of this country. But since it must subsist for our shame, let it subsist for our instruction."[5]

About this time (1780) there were few public men who exhibited either the courage or the inclination to defend the English Catholics as a body, or individually. And as these instances of prominent

[1] *Dolman's Magazine*, vol. v. p. 81.
[2] Husenbeth's *Life of Bishop Milner*.   [3] Oliver's *Collections*, p. 24.
[4] Shaw's *History of Stoke-on-Trent*, 1843.   [5] Edmund Burke.

men "guilty" of saying a word in favor of Catholics were rare, it is equally just and fair to mention at least one notable exception. The mob in the Gordon riots attacked persons on the mere suspicion of being friendly to the Catholics. It has also been demonstrated that the Church of England was, through her ministers and supporters, a thoroughgoing opponent to the toleration (if not existence) of the Catholics. One Anglican bishop there was, however, whose courage was much greater than that of many of his colleagues and brethren in the ministry of a lesser degree.

In 1781 the Bishop of London (Dr. Porteous) opposed an effort "to lay such restrictions on the Catholics as would prevent their increase".[1] That was no doubt a step in the direction of tolerance, and, at the same time, indicates most eloquently the prevailing desire to prevent "increase" in any shape whatever.

The eighteenth century was most prolific in the production of some of England's greatest writers, but how few were there, comparatively speaking, inclined to take sides with their persecuted fellow-citizens! There is, however, one figure in the world of letters that stands out in bold relief, and that figure was the renowned Dr. Samuel Johnson. That great man was, without question, one of the most remarkable literary men of the period. He was an earnest and loyal supporter of his own Church, but he was an equally earnest hater of hypocrisy, cant, and oppression. Boswell, his faithful biographer, says of him: "He argued in defence of the peculiar tenets of the Church of Rome. He had a great respect for the 'old religion,' as the mild Melancthon calls that of the Roman Catholic Church." This respect he showed in many of his conversations. Sir Wm. Scott informed Boswell he heard Johnson say: "A man who is converted from Protestantism to Popery may be sincere: he parts with nothing: he is only superadding to what he already had. But a convert from Popery to Protestantism gives up much of what he has held as sacred as anything he retains. There is so much *laceration of mind* in such a conversion that it can hardly be sincere and lasting." Johnson, notwithstanding his great learning, was in error on many points of Catholic doctrine, but he was better informed than many of his contemporaries. Many public men of the time did not take the trouble to acquaint themselves with the principles of the Catholic religion, and we can well imagine the scorn with which Johnson

---

[1] Dr. Beard's *Biographical Dictionary*. London: Cassell, 1851.

would have regarded the puerility exhibited by Pitt, the statesman who desired to know if Catholics were justified "in not keeping faith with heretics". Though there was much in the Catholic religion which Johnson condemned, he was by no means an entire believer in the thirty-nine articles. Of purgatory and the mass he declared himself in the following dialogue: "I proceeded: 'What do you think, sir, of purgatory as believed by the Roman Catholics?' Johnson: 'Why, sir, it is a very harmless doctrine. They are of opinion that the generality of mankind are neither so obstinately wicked as to deserve everlasting punishment, nor so good as to merit being admitted into the society of blessed spirits; and, therefore, that God is graciously pleased to allow of a middle state, where they may be purified by certain degrees of suffering. You see, sir, there is nothing unreasonable in this.' Boswell: 'But then, sir, their masses for the dead?' Johnson: 'Why, sir, if it be once established that there are souls in purgatory, it is as proper to pray for *them* as for our brethren of mankind who are yet in this life'. Boswell: 'The idolatry of the mass?' Johnson: 'Sir, there is no idolatry in the mass. They believe God to be there, and they adore Him.'" When we consider the position of the Catholics at that time it will be reasonable and correct to deduce therefrom that there were few conversions to the Church. We read, however, in Boswell's great work that about 1784 "Mrs. Kennicot spoke of her brother, the Reverend Mr. Chamberlayne, who had given up great prospects in the Church of England on his conversion to the Roman Catholic faith. Johnson, who warmly admired every man who acted from a conscientious regard to principle, erroneous or not, exclaimed fervently: 'God bless him'."[1]

On one occasion Johnson said: "I shall never be a Papist, unless on the near approach of death, of which I have a very great terror".[2] Johnson, however, when death came, had no fear; and he died a sincere member of the Anglican Church. Though opposed to crudeness and innovation, he was in many matters in advance of the times in which he lived, and particularly on the now accepted constitutional principle of liberty of conscience.

[1] The quotations here given on Johnson are from Boswell's *Life of Johnson*.
[2] Compare this with Lord Byron's saying: "I often wish I had been born a Catholic".

Another remarkable man who lived and worked during the greater part of the last century was John Wesley. We have already seen how Catholics, Dissenters, and Methodists were persecuted; but, as a rule, Catholics were visited with much greater severity than other bodies. This persecution was chiefly due to the ignorance of the people and the example set by their teachers, who, if they did not openly countenance attacks, showed by their silence tacit approval thereof. Considering this, it is singular to find a man like Wesley, who in his own person was frequently persecuted, the possessor of narrow principles. Whilst he clamoured for toleration to be extended to his party, he was by no means tolerant either to the Catholic Church or to Catholics. Wesley was a remarkable man, and no doubt enthusiastic. He saw the torpor that prevailed in his own Church, and he strove by revivalistic methods to bring about a change; until by degrees he became the founder of what is to-day a powerful organisation. It is questionable whether there can be found in the records of English literature, or that of any other country, any parallel to equal the feat of Wesley, who, for the long period of fifty-five years, kept an almost continuous record of work done. His *Journal* is most interesting, not only as a history of the prevailing manners, but also as a topographical sketch of the United Kingdom between the years 1735 and 1790. But that autobiography is considerably marred by the self-laudatory style which prevails from beginning to end; and it may be summed up as a book of Wesley on Wesley. The Catholics he always alludes to as "Papists" or "Romanists," coupled with a style which is contemptuous and patronising, and by no means befitting the character of an evangelist, for it is in that light he is regarded by many. The Bull *Unigenitus* of Pope Benedict XIV. Mr. Wesley designated "diabolical".[1]

The prosecution of priests for illegal offences—viz., the celebration of mass—was persisted in until late in the last century. A Catholic writer has a comment on this, wherein he states that " Charles Butler tells us that the single house of Dynely & Ashmalls, attorneys in Gray's Inn, had defended more than twenty priests under such prosecution for offences (under the *Penal Code*); and instances are on record as late as 1782 of Catholics being fined and

---

[1] "That diabolical Bull *Unigenitus*, which destroys the very foundation of Christianity."—Wesley's *Journal*, 11th January, 1750.

distrained for refusing to attend the services of the Established Church.[1]

In a previous chapter we have alluded to the services rendered by another distinguished Protestant and Member of the British Parliament—Edmund Burke. But there is still another quotation which will tend to illustrate the condition of English Catholics at this period. The condition of the clergy was this: "The clergy, concealed in garrets in private houses or obliged to take a shelter (hardly safe to themselves, but infinitely dangerous to their country) under the privileges of foreign ministers, officiated as their servants and under their protection. The whole body of the Catholics condemned to beggary and to ignorance in their native land have been obliged to learn the principle of letters at the hazard of all other principles from the charity of your enemies. . . . It is but six or seven years since a clergyman of the name of Malony, a man of morals, neither guilty nor accused of anything noxious to the State, was condemned to perpetual imprisonment for exercising the functions of his religion; and after lying in jail two or three years was relieved by the mercy of a Government from perpetual imprisonment, on condition of perpetual banishment. A brother of the Earl of Shrewsbury, a Talbot—a name respectable in this country, whilst its glory is any part of its concern—was hauled to the bar of the Old Bailey, among common felons, and only escaped the same doom, either by some error in the process, or that the wretch who brought him there could not correctly describe his person, I now forget which."[2]

It was only by technical omissions that a Catholic could retain his or her property. Even Catholic ladies were not safe in their possessions, for says Burke in his great speech: "It was but the other day that a lady of condition beyond the middle of life was on the point of being stripped of her whole fortune by a near relation to whom she had been a friend and benefactor; and she must have been totally ruined, without a power of redress or mitigation from the courts of law, had not the legislature itself rushed in, and by a special Act of Parliament rescued her from the injustice of its own statutes". From the foregoing quotation we may easily sum up the condition of Catholics up to the year 1791, when some toleration of a miserably narrow character was meted out.

---

[1] Flanagan's *British and Irish History*, p. 792. London, 1851.
[2] Burke's Speech to the Electors of Bristol.

CHAPTER VIII.

THE "TOLERATION ACT" OF 1791.

ONE hundred years ago—in the year 1791—may be said to have been inaugurated the beginning of the end of Catholic persecution. Two centuries had passed by since the Catholics had begun to feel anew the iron heel of oppression. It may have been felt by those in authority at the period we now write of that surely the time had arrived when the Crown and the established religion were safe from the effects of Romanism. Whether, as is contended by some eminent authorities,[1] the Act of Toleration was brought about by the "protestations" of the Catholics is questionable. It would be preferable, and doubtless more correct, to attribute the passing of the measure to the growing liberality of the times, slow as was that growth. The Act was, however, passed, but it was of a negative character. It became law forty years before the emancipation period, and although it did not extend to Catholics the full rights of citizenship, it defined for them what was *not* penal, and one effect was that it took away the lucrative positions hitherto held by the common informer. Doubtless the Catholics of the period regarded it as a great boon, and such it was, when we consider the persecutions they had previously endured. This Act, commonly called the Toleration Act (31 Geo. III. c. 22), provides that an oath of allegiance therein stated may be taken by Roman Catholics. This oath was of a most insulting character, containing as it did the following "safeguards" for the preservation of the Protestant religion and society generally: "And I do swear that I do reject and detest, as an unchristian and impious principle, that it is lawful to murder or destroy any person or persons whatsoever, for or under pretence of their being infidels or heretics; and also, that unchristian and impious principle that faith is not to be kept with infidels or heretics; and I do declare that I do not believe that the Pope of Rome, or any other foreign prince, prelate, State, or potentate, hath or ought to have any temporal or civil jurisdiction within this realm". To ensure the continuance of existing institutions the oath declared, testified, and protested as follows: "And I do solemnly . . . testify and declare, that I do make this declaration . . . without any evasion, equivocation, or mental reservation whatever; and without any dispensation already granted by

---

[1] Such as Mr. Gladstone. See pamphlets *Vatican Decrees*, &c.

the Pope, or any authority of the See of Rome," &c., &c. Persons taking the oath were exempt from the penalties inflicted by various Acts of Elizabeth, James I., Charles I., and Charles II., William III., Anne, George I., and George II., " on recusants or reputed Papists, seminary priests, and other such disobedient persons ". The third and fourth clauses provided that all Catholics taking the oath of allegiance should be exempt from all penalties for hearing or saying mass or performing any religious service in their places of worship, or for being a priest or member of a religious order, or for entering any such order, provided that such places of Catholic worship are duly certified to the Justices of the Peace at Quarter Sessions. Provided also that such places of worship have not steeples and bells, and that such ecclesiastics shall not wear their vestments or habits out of their churches, or in a private house where not more than five persons are assembled."[1]

[1] See also Madden's *Penal Laws*, &c.

John Lingard, D.D., the well-known Catholic historian, was born at Winchester, February 1, 1771, and being destined for the priesthood was sent to the English College of Douai, in France, where he remained till that college, in common with most of the religious establishments of France, was broken up by the troubles of the Revolution. In consequence of the Catholic Relief Bill enabling Catholics to open schools in England, the Douai community was transferred to Crookhall, and ultimately to Ushaw, in the county of Durham. Lingard continued attached to the college in its several migrations, although not always resident. In 1793 he accepted the office of tutor in the family of Lord Stourton; but in the following year he returned to complete his theological studies at Crookhall, where he entered into priest's orders, and where he continued as professor of philosophy, prefect of studies, and vice-president, until 1810, when he was named president. In 1811, however, he accepted the humble cure of Hornby, near Lancaster, in which he continued to reside till his death, July 13, 1851. Lingard's first important work was the *Antiquity of the Anglo-Saxon Church* (8vo, 1806), reprinted in 1810, and afterwards, in a much-enlarged edition (2 vols., 1845). This was but the pioneer of what became eventually the labor of his life—a *History of England* (6 vols., 4to) published at intervals 1819-1825; and afterwards in 14 vols. 8vo, 1823-1831. This work before the death of the author had passed through six editions. From its first appearance it attracted much attention, as being founded on original authorities and the result of much new research. It was criticised with considerable asperity in its polemical bearings; but the author, in his replies, displayed so much erudition, and so careful a consideration of the original authorities, that the result was to add materially to his reputation as a scholar and a critic. It won for itself a place as a work of original research, and although it bears unmistakable evidence of the religious opinions of the author, yet there is also evidence of a sincere desire to investigate and to ascertain the truth of history. In recognition of his great services many honors were offered to him and a pension of £300 from the Crown. His remains were interred in his old college of St. Cuthbert, at Ushaw.

[Mr. J. Orlebar Payne, in his work *Old English Catholic Missions*, p. 13, states that the *Catholic Directory* for 1793 explains the Toleration Act of 1791, " but warns gentlemen returning from abroad that the 'importer or receiver of such things as crosses, pictures, *ladies' missals*, rosaries, breviaries, &c., alike incur a *præmunire !*' Such then," adds Mr. Payne, "were the magnificent first-fruits of the 'Catholic Relief Acts'."]

Without doubt the oath contained expressions and denials derogatory to the dignity of any respectable citizen, but it must be remembered that the Catholics were at that time looked upon as a class whose word was not worthy of reliance except in the form of an oath. Hence, although the Catholics protested too much, no blame can be attached to them. They were a handful of people " (enough to torment but not enough to fear), perhaps not so many of both sexes and of all ages as fifty thousand ".

CHAPTER IX.

THE POSITION OF CATHOLICS DURING THE LATTER YEARS OF THE EIGHTEENTH CENTURY AND THE EARLY PORTION OF THE NINETEENTH.

VARIOUS are the pictures of the condition of Catholics during the eighteenth century and the first decade of the present century. The ministrations of religion were not at times carried out without experiencing great difficulties. For instance, the Catholics at Horton, in Gloucestershire, were attended from Bath, a distance of fifteen miles, from 1795 until 1815 " during the eight Indulgences". Father Bridsale, so late as the year 1815, said Mass at Horton in the upper chamber of a poor cottage ; the room was ten feet long by nine, with scarcely head room between him and the thatch. A deal table was used for the altar, and the wind blew through the broken panes of the window ; about nine or ten persons assembled.

In connection with the efforts for emancipation may be here mentioned the following : The new House of Commons met 19th December, 1806, and the Whigs introduced the Catholic Bill by the hands of Mr. Grey, afterwards Lord Howick. On the 13th March following it began to be rumored that the King had changed his mind about the Catholic Bill. Lord Howick (subsequently Lord Grey) actually withdrew the bill on the 18th March. It was put forward as a reason for the withdrawal of the bill that an attempt had been made to force the King to break his coronation oath!

In 1820 the present church at Moorfields was finished. The Papal treasury and sacristy were at that time very empty, but Pius VII. ordered the most valuable object in church plate which he possessed to be prepared for a present. His attendants remarked that it was the most costly thing he had, and his reply was: "There is nothing too good for me to give the English Catholics". The late Cardinal Wiseman, in his work[1] from which the above paragraph is quoted, has the following note: "May 1. The King of England has written in Latin to the Pope, with his sign manual: the first instance of such a correspondence since our Revolution (1688). The Pope is pleased, and is answering it." The year 1824 developed in the counties of Devon and Cornwall an improved state of affairs for the Catholic body, as we learn from a Catholic publication of that year. This paper[2] has the following: "Upon the whole the actual state of religion and the prospect before us should be deemed encouraging. The number of chapels has increased, and are well attended. Much progress has been made towards the decent maintenance of the clergy. The tide of prejudice against our religion and its ministers is visibly on the ebb. This change of public opinion is partly owing to the diffusion of education among all classes and the frequent discussion of the Catholic question in both Houses of Parliament." In 1828 the Test and Corporation Acts were repealed. Five years later (1833) were commenced the "Tracts for the Times," a religious movement full of interest to the Church and its members.

The Marriage Act, which made "legal the marriage of Catholics by the priests of their Church," came into operation 1st July, 1837. Prior to that period, Catholics were not legally married, so far as the religious element was concerned, except by a minister of the Church of England. In 1838 there were only 197 places registered for the celebration of marriages in "Roman Catholic chapels," and for this privilege a tax of three pounds per chapel was levied. It may be of interest to note that at the end of the year 1863 the number of churches on the register for the solemnisation of marriages presented a total of 587. In 1890 the number compiled from the official records is given as 895.

[1] *Recollections of the Four Last Popes.*
[2] *Catholic Spectator*, March, 1824.

The Catholic Institute was formed in 1839, the object of which was, as stated in the prospectus, " to expose the falsehood of the calumnious charges made against the Catholic religion, to defend the real tenets of Catholicity, and the circulation of all useful knowledge on the above-mentioned subjects ".

CHAPTER X.

CATHOLIC DIFFERENCES.[1]

IN the history of the religions of the world, and particularly as regards the Christian Churches, no system has suffered less from internal discord than has the Catholic Church. The reason for this is not far to seek, nor difficult to comprehend. The Catholic Church is an institution founded by God ; and, therefore, not subject to error such as that which prevails in religious systems outside the Church, inasmuch as these latter are the work of men. From the very beginning of Christianity the Church has had to confront error. Witness the Arian[2] heresy, which St. Athanasius arose to combat. Then there were the Nestorians ;[3] and, later, the Albigenses.[4] The so-called Reformation owed its origin to such men as Wicklif, Luther,[5] and Henry VIII. King Henry, before he became a persecutor, was a defender of the

[1] " The Catholic Church in England maintains as its highest endowment its divine independence, indicated by endurance of spoliation, and of three centuries of oppression."—Cardinal Manning, *Dublin Review*, 1885.

[2] The Arian heresy was condemned by the Council of Nice in the fourth century.

[3] The Nestorian teachings were condemned by the Council of Ephesus in the fifth century.

[4] St. Dominic, as is well known, preached successfully against the Albigensian heresies.

[5] In an article on " A Jansenist Dictionary," Isaac D'Israeli, in his wonderful book, the *Curiosities of Literature*, has the following estimate of the character of Luther : "The furious Luther, perceiving himself assisted by the credit of several princes, broke loose against the Church with the most inveterate rage, and raising the most terrible alarm against the Pope. . . . Nothing equals the rage of this phrenetic man, who was not satisfied with exhaling his fury in horrid declamations, but who was for putting all in practice. He raised his excesses to the height by inveighing against the vow of chastity, and in marrying publicly Catherine de Bore, a nun, whom he enticed with eight others from their convents. He had prepared the minds of the people for this infamous proceeding by a treatise, which he entitled *Examples of the Papistical Doctrine*

Faith, a fact so historically true as to remain engraven on the English coinage of to-day.

But the real groundwork of opposition to the Church lay either in self-love or want of submission to authority.

The history of religion in England outside the Catholic Church is the history of schism, dissent, difference. When the Catholic Church was put down by force in England, there was placed in its stead a State Church, to suit the crotchets of rulers and latitudinarians. That Church since its foundation has had its divisions, its schools of thought, its parties. All of these have their "views" upon the fundamental principles of Christianity; from Baptism to the doctrine of the Real Presence, from Penance to Holy Orders and Matrimony. To such an extent is that Church torn and distracted that the appointment of a bishop, vicar or curate is invariably made a matter of consideration as to the "views" on given points held by the person sought to be appointed. Then in this country we had the spectacle of seceders from the secessionists, who went to form the revivalistic bodies known as "Dissenters". This term is somewhat of an anomaly, when we consider that the State Church is equally an institution dissenting from the Universal Church. The dissenters then in turn had their dissidents, and new religious bodies were set up, so that in our own time England has sects more numerous than any other nation on the face of the earth.[1] Such is the consequence of separation from that Church which is to teach the truth for all time, "even to the consummation of the world".

In examining the history of the Catholic Church in this country from 1690, it is desirable that the question be dealt with: Has the Church during that period been subject to internal dissensions? If so, why, and to what extent?

---

and Theology, in which he condemns the praises which all the saints had given to continence." Much that Luther wrote is of so vile a character as to preclude quotation here. As a mild specimen, however, of the style of the "Reformer," we give the following: "The Papists are all asses, and will always remain asses. Put them in whatever sauce you choose—boiled, roasted, fried, skinned, beat, hashed—they are always the same asses." Again: "What a pleasing sight would it be to see the Pope and the cardinals hanging on one gallows, in exact order like the seals which dangle from the Bulls of the Pope. What an excellent council they would hold under the gallows!"

[1] Dr. Di Bruno in his *Catholic Belief* (1883) states that the Registrar-General gives a list of more than one hundred and eighty religious divisions in England and Wales having registered places of worship.

The Catholic differences, which, it may be remarked at the outset, were political in character rather than religious, commenced in the year 1783. This was five years after the passing of the small measure of relief to the Catholics which led up to the Gordon riots. The Catholic Committee was at first constituted of five persons, whose object was to " promote the affairs of Roman Catholics in England ". The chief measure of the committee was a plan to procure the appointment of Bishops in ordinary, instead of Vicars-Apostolic. In the opinion of Dr. Milner and others such action tended in the direction of lay interference. The committee proceeded further, and in May, 1783, drew up a paper containing assertions injurious to the spiritual government of the Vicars-Apostolic. In 1787 the committee addressed a letter to the Catholics of England, in one part of which there was a statement to the effect that the people had an equal authority with the pastors in regulating every part of the Church discipline, and that they were competent to make whatever changes they pleased in conformity with the laws of the State. Subsequently, a memorial was presented to Mr. Pitt, setting forth the grievances under which the Catholics labored, and expressing a desire for that statesman's support in the intended application for redress.

In the following year (1788) the committee resolved that their secretary (Mr. Charles Butler) should prepare a bill for the repeal of laws against the Catholics, and this was accompanied by a declaration of principles, known as the *Protestation*. This was signed by certain prelates and influential Catholics, but with the assurance that it would not be followed by any new oath. The committee, however, notwithstanding this, soon framed an oath, containing new provisions, in which they adopted the extraordinary title of " Protesting Catholic Dissenters ".[1] This oath was formally condemned and declared unlawful to be taken by the unanimous decision of the four Vicars-Apostolic—viz., Bishops Walmesley, James Talbot, Thos. Talbot, and Gibson—at a meeting held at Hammersmith, 19th October, 1789, and they published their condemnation in the form of an encyclical letter to the faithful, in which they declared that no oath affecting religion could be taken without the approbation of the Bishops, and their lordships added: " To this determination, therefore, we require your submission ".

In the course of the same year several pamphlets on the vexed

---

[1] See Mr. Gladstone's remarks on this in *Vatican Decrees*, &c.

question in debate were written on both sides by the committee and Dr. Milner.

On the 19th January, 1791, the condemnation of the oath previously made by the Bishops was ratified by the Holy See, and in the summer of the same year a clergyman of the Benedictine Order was suspended for advocacy of the committee's views.

In the month of April, 1792, there was an attempt made to settle the differences between the Bishops and the Oaths Committee. The committee published a " buff book," but still adhered to the " protest," and denied the right of the Vicars-Apostolic to condemn an oath or any other measure which they (the Vicars-Apostolic) might declare to be of a spiritual nature without showing the grounds of their censure, and repeated their determination " to resist any ecclesiastical interference which might militate against the freedom of English Catholics ".

From this period (1792) up to the year 1810 there appears to have been a cessation of the internecine warfare ; but on January 31, 1810, a few Catholic noblemen met and drew up a series of resolutions to be brought forward the following day. The fifth resolution read as follows :—

" That the English Roman Catholics are firmly persuaded that adequate provision for the maintenance of the civil and religious establishments of this kingdom may be made consistently with the strictest adherence on their part to the tenets and discipline of the Roman Catholic religion ; and that any arrangement founded on this basis of mutual satisfaction and security, and extending to them the full enjoyment of the civil constitution of their country, will meet with their grateful concurrence ".

The wording of this resolution gave rise to much controversy, and Dr. Milner (who in the year 1813 had been made Bishop of the Midland District) contended that the object of the resolution was to " alter our Church discipline by giving up the rights of bishops ".

The parties responsible for the resolution stoutly defended it,[1] contending that it was in no way inconsistent with the Catholic religion. Two bishops signed the paper, considering it " harmless and free from danger ". In the following year (1811) Mr. Charles Butler issued letters in defence, and Bishop Milner published replies thereto.

---

[1] Butler's *Historical Memoirs of English Catholics*, 3rd edit., p. 168.

On the 19th February, 1813, a meeting of the committee was held in London, there being present several Catholic noblemen. The real business of the meeting was to "establish an understanding between laity, clergy, and bishops, who had been exposed to obloquy since 1791". On the last day of April, 1813, Mr. Grattan brought in his Bill for Catholic Emancipation, which was read a second time on 11th May. In the opinion of Bishop Milner, the bill contained some objectionable clauses. On 24th May, when the bill went into committee, an amendment was moved that the words in the first clause, "to sit and vote in either House of Parliament," should be omitted. This was carried by a majority of four only, but denuded of this principle for which the Catholics had so long struggled, the bill was worthless, and it was not proceeded with. Exactly sixteen years from this date the Catholics received emancipation without sacrificing a single principle derogatory to the dignity of their religion or citizenship.

So ended this unfortunate controversy. In calmly surveying this purely "Catholic question," after a lapse of generations, we may reasonably be surprised at the agitation it caused. On the one hand there was an influential body of gentlemen who sought to better the laws under which the Catholics labored. This committee was composed of men of great ability, such as Mr. Charles Butler, a man of learning, the author of several works; and acting with him were some members of the Catholic aristocracy, and even a few ecclesiastics. That their motives were in many respects praiseworthy will be admitted, but that they were in some degree dangerous will be equally conceded. They were moved to action by the degrading condition under which their fellow-Catholics labored. Undoubtedly the desire of the committee, and those prominent Catholics who acted with them, was to ameliorate the condition of the Catholics of England, but in so doing they assented to principles undignified in character, and principles which sooner or later would have been felt as most galling by the Catholic body. True it is, they lived and acted when Catholics were looked upon as aliens, and when "protestations" were considered by an ignorant people requisite for the slightest concession.

On the other hand the majority of the bishops, priests, and people were inclined to accept no boon, however tempting, wherein the sacrifice of a single religious principle was involved. That their attitude was directed by a wise foresight subsequent events confirmed. Of that period we may say " all's well that ends well," and keen as was the controversy it created no schism, and the worst that can be said of it is that there was an exhibition of over-officiousness on the part of the committee.

The condition of the Catholics at the beginning of the present century must also be considered. Comparing that period with the present, we may conclude that to-day there is reason for thankfulness; the Catholics are now free and unfettered, and there is no need for the surrender of any political or other principle. To-day there is nothing incompatible with citizenship, so far as the Catholic religion is concerned. We shall also learn from the past that to the Bishops as the divinely appointed guardians of the people may safely be entrusted all matters affecting the Catholic Church, and the spiritual well-being of the people over whom they have been placed by Divine authority.

CHAPTER XI.

BRIEF HISTORY OF CATHOLIC EMANCIPATION.

THE history of Catholic Emancipation, like other events chronicled in this work, is the history of an object not achieved without considerable agitation on the part of the Catholic body. The term itself conveys to the mind the meaning of the movement. Before 1829 the Catholics were politically in a state of bondage, and from this they were " emancipated," just as later British slaves were emancipated from the thraldom with which, on account of race and color, they were visited. During the latter part of the eighteenth century the efforts of the Catholic body were directed rather to the repeal of penal measures bearing directly on their religion than to any action such as a claim to the elective franchise. The actual period of the agitation in which the claim for the franchise was put forward may be said to have commenced in 1805. In that year Lord Grenville introduced a motion into the House of Lords for a committee to be formed for the simple consideration of what was called the " Catholic Question ". This was defeated by 178 to 49. From that time there were year by year no fewer than thirty-two motions and bills introduced into either House for ameliorative measures for Catholics until the achievement of 1829. The humiliating condition of the Catholic body in the year 1810 was well expressed by Mr. Wyndham, who, on presenting the petition of the Catholics to the House of Commons, said: "When I speak of the obscurity of the English Roman Catholics I do not mean that they are destitute of hereditary virtues and hereditary dignities. I cannot contemplate a more noble and affecting spectacle than an ancient Roman Catholic gentleman, in the midst of his people, exercising the virtue of beneficence, humanity, and hospitality. If they are obscure, it is because they are proscribed as aliens in the State; because they are shut out from this assembly, where many of those who are far less worthy are allowed to sit. . . . Have they ever attempted to obtain their rights either by clamor or by servility? On the contrary, their conduct has proved that no other body is more justly entitled to respect and admiration."

In 1813 an important measure, framed with this intention (the removal of Catholic disabilities), was defeated in the Commons by only four votes.

Describing the condition of English Catholics in 1813, a writer[1] says: "Catholics cannot sit in Parliament or hold any office under Government, be admitted into any corporation or presented to any benefice. Priests not allowed the celebration of their rites, but agreeably to the restrictions of the English Act 31 George III. Catholic schoolmasters cannot take Protestant scholars, neither can professors endow a school or college for education of their children in the faith. Catholic soldiers, by the Annual Mutiny Act, refusing to frequent Church of England worship when ordered to do so, are liable to the penalty of one shilling, and to be laid in irons for twelve hours. Catholics are prevented from voting at elections."

Among these efforts some were successful, viz., May 9, 1817, a bill for opening the army to English Catholics, relieving the Catholic officers from the penalty of not taking the Oath of Supremacy. In 1821 a bill was introduced, passed through the Lower House, for the extension of the franchise to the Catholics, but it was rejected by the Peers. The lowest point of degradation seemed to have been reached on the 17th April, 1823, when upon the motion of Mr. Plunkett for a committee on the Catholic claims, Sir Francis Burdett rose and said with perfect truth: "The annual discussion of the question has become a farce". The session of

---

[1] *Historical Account of the Laws Enacted against Catholics*, by J. B. Browne: London, 1813.

the same year witnessed an effort made to raise the English Catholics to an equality with the Irish Catholics. Both were degraded by the existing state of the law; but there were degrees of degradation, and the English Catholics stood on the lowest step. Amongst the members of their faith they could count the noblest in the land, and they could claim men distinguished for their talents, their learning, and their virtues. "Not even the lowest situation in the Excise could be had in Great Britain without qualifying by abjuring Popery." On the 28th May, 1823, Lord Nugent, without consulting the English Catholics, introduced a motion in the House of Commons for leave to bring in a bill which would place the Roman Catholics of England and Scotland in the same position with respect to civil rights and franchise as the Catholics of Ireland.

In 1824 a small but restricted modicum of relief was granted to enable the Duke of Norfolk to exercise the office of Earl Marshal, and a bill relieving English Catholics of the double land tax. The Catholics were grateful for small mercies. At a meeting of the British Catholic Association,[1] held 26th June, 1824, it was "moved by the Earl of Shrewsbury, seconded by the Hon. Hugh Clifford, and resolved unanimously, 'that this committee do offer their sincere congratulations to his Grace the Duke of Norfolk on his recent admission to perform in person the functions of his high hereditary office of Earl Marshal of England; which they consider not alone as a well-merited tribute, paid to his exalted rank and private virtues, but also as bearing ample testimony to the growing liberty of the times'".

In 1825 there was introduced into the House of Commons a Bill to provide " for the removal of the disqualifications under which His Majesty's Roman Catholic subjects now labor". This also was defeated. In 1826 a general election took place. The Whigs adopted the Catholic Question, but in the city of London the "no-Popery" cry was raised against Alderman Wood, an emancipator.

On 5th January, 1827, the great opponent of the Catholic claims (the Duke of York) expired, and on the 17th February the illness of the Earl of Liverpool led to the dissolution of his administrations. An indication of the prevalence of a better feel-

---

[1] The British Catholic Association contained such well-known names as the Duke of Norfolk, Earl of Shrewsbury, Lord Stourton, Sir E. Blount, Bart., Hon. H. Clifford, William Vaughan, P. T. Townley, E. Blount, &c. Branches were established in Manchester, Preston, Birmingham, Liverpool, Blackburn, and Wigan.

ing with regard to the Catholic claims was manifested on March 5 of the same year. Sir F. Burdett submitted a motion to the House of Commons to take into consideration the laws inflicting penalties on His Majesty's Roman Catholic subjects, with a view of removing them. The motion was rejected by four votes only. In 1828 further progress was made by the abrogation of the Test and Corporation Acts. On May 8, 1828, a resolution pledging the House to a favorable consideration of the Catholic claims was proposed, and after three nights' debate carried by a majority of six. Sir R. Peel on this occasion " prophesied " that the removal of these disabilities would be attended with a danger to the Protestant religion. The resolution passed in the Commons was communicated to the Lords on May 16, and on June 9 they rejected it by a majority of forty-four. The Duke of Wellington declared that "the securities which we now enjoy, and which for a length of time we have enjoyed, are indispensable to the safety of Church and State ".[1]

The position of English Catholics in the year 1828 was ably stated in a work produced by a Catholic peer,[2] the Earl of Shrewsbury, who wrote : " Catholics are only known to the Constitution for the purposes of pains and penalties. We are worse than aliens in our native land, inasmuch as an alien is under the protection of equal laws, which we are not. Witness, among others, the decisions, in 1825, of the Lords in Council upon the claims of the British Catholics for the restoration of their confiscated property, by which, though the money was actually paid by the Government of France, it was not permitted to reach its destination, under the plea that it would be employed in superstitious uses." In another portion of the same work the Earl wrote : " We still suffer in our privileges and our rights, and even in our fortunes, witness the double land tax,[3] while our reputation, both as subjects and as Christians, is still loaded with the defamation of nearly three centuries ".

At length in 1829 came the final triumph. We need scarcely do more than recapitulate the various stages for the relief of

---

[1] *Parliamentary Debates*, vol. xix.

[2] *Reasons for Not Taking the Test; for Not Conforming to the Established Church*, &c., by John, Earl of Shrewsbury, p. 12. London : Booker, 1828.

[3] Whilst this work was passing through the press, Mr. G. Banks introduced into the House of Commons a bill for relieving the Catholics from the penalty of double assessment of the land tax.

His Majesty's Catholic subjects. On February 5 the speech from the throne recommended the propriety of considering the Catholic claims. On March 5 Sir Robert Peel (who had rapidly changed his views) brought on his motion for a Committee on the Catholic question, the result being—ayes, 348; noes, 160. On the same day a bill was introduced for the abolition of civil disabilities by repealing the Oaths of Supremacy and Abjuration, and substituting an Oath of Allegiance. The bill also rendered Catholics eligible to certain offices, but excluded the Chancellorship. On March 30, on the third reading of the bill, it was carried, the numbers being—for, 327; against, 146. On April 4 the bill passed the House of Lords by 147 contents against 79 non-contents, not counting proxies.[1]

CHAPTER XII.

STATISTICS AS TO THE POSITION OF THE CATHOLIC CHURCH IN ENGLAND AND WALES FROM 1690 TO 1840.

THE absence of proof as to the number of Catholics in England and Wales from 1690 to 1767 may easily be accounted for. This want of information is an addition, if any were needed, of the arguments in the preceding pages, viz., that the Catholic body for close upon a hundred years were visited in the most severe manner by penal enactments. William III., as a matter of policy no doubt, thought fit to procure a kind of census, with a view, it may reasonably be supposed, to find out the number of *probable* opponents. But from the time of William down to the seventh year of George III., the Catholics as a body were not apparently of sufficient importance to be recognised; they were regarded as a small sect to be hunted, and worthy only of the rigorous laws passed for their debasement. On the death of William, according to the testimony of Sir John Dalrymple, there was found in an

---

[1] Protests against the Relief Bill were entered in the Journal of the House of Lords by thirty peers and one bishop. During the discussion of this measure the House of Lords received against the bill 2521 petitions, and in favor of it 1014. In the House of Commons there were 2013 petitions against the bill, and in favor of it 955. Total petitions for the bill, 1969; against, 4534—majority against, 2565. According to the *Atlas* newspaper of April 19, 1829, of the English newspaper press of that period there were 107 in favor of emancipation, 87 against it, and 44 neutral.—Madden's *Penal Laws*, p. 310.

iron chest belonging to that monarch a document showing the number of Catholics in England and Wales to be 13,856, viz., in the province of Canterbury 11,878, and in the province of York 1978.[1]

As to any record of the number of clergy or churches, there is none whatever. Such a record could not be compiled because the clergy were regarded as felons, and although there were some few churches " tolerated," they were by no means looked upon as were other buildings. They were allowed on sufferance.

For more than seventy years, therefore, the Catholics as a body were ignored, and not considered of sufficient importance for any Parliamentary return as to their numbers.

In the year 1767, however, a return was made, in which it was shown that the number of Catholics in England and Wales was 67,916; and in 1780 a return to the House of Lords gave the number as 69,376, showing an increase of 1460. In the same year there were 359 priests in the four districts—viz., London District, 58; Western, 44; Midland, 90; and in the Northern District, 167.

Of this period, and in regard to the last-named district, some interesting statistics are given by a writer on Catholic progress in an article recently published.[2]

From that article we glean the following: " Bishop Gibson, the Vicar-Apostolic of the Northern District, sent to ' Hilton,' as he called it in the phraseology of the persecution days—that is to say, to Rome—on January 8, 1787, the following ' computation of Catholic missioners': In Lancashire there were 23,000 communicants. He gives the clergy of Lancashire, secular and regular, as 62. As to the other counties in the district, Bishop Gibson gives to Yorkshire 4512 communicants and 41 priests. The four counties now constituting the diocese of Hexham and Newcastle had in all 5506 communicants and 35 priests. Cheshire had 340 communicants and three priests."

---

[1] This statement as to numbers is partly correct, but not wholly so, though the figures have been relied on by many Catholic writers, and frequently quoted. The following statement will, however, place beyond doubt the actual number of Catholics at the period referred to: "A return presented to William III. divides the freeholders of England and Wales as follows: Conformists, 2,477,254; Nonconformists, 108,676; Papists, 13,856; total, 2,599,786; and the number of *persons* of the Roman Catholic faith is said to be only 27,696". It will thus be seen that the number of freeholders had been accepted as the actual number of Catholics (Census of 1851).

[2] Article in *The Month*, March, 1891, by Father Morris.

These statistics bear out the statement as to the paucity of the Catholics of this country a little over a century ago. The Northern District had at that time, as it has to-day, a large proportion of the clergy.

In 1785 there were about 170 private chapels, and a public chapel in each of the following towns: Worcester (built in 1685), Wolverhampton (1743), Preston (1761), Shrewsbury (1764), Cobridge (1780), Garstang (1784). There were also chapels in Manchester, Newcastle-on-Tyne, Norwich, and Liverpool. The number for London between 1780 and 1790 is not given. St. George's, Southwark, was built in 1786. In 1791 the Rev. Mr. Griffiths appealed in the *Directory* for £1200 " for the chapel in St. George's Fields ".[1] The *Directory* of 1793 gives a list of 18 "chapels in or near London". It was in this year that a few Catholic chapels (recognised as the chapels of ambassadors) first appeared in the *Directory*.

The Midland District, over which the learned Dr. Milner was for some years Vicar-Apostolic, consisted of fifteen counties. The biographer of that great prelate has in his work[2] the following:—

" The total number of Catholics in England and Wales, by the returns made to the House of Lords in 1780, was 69,376. In twenty-three years, up to 1803, they may have increased to more than 70,000. Nearly half of this number were included in the Northern District alone, as the Catholics of Lancashire far outnumbered those in every other county. The London District ranked next in numbers, and the remainder were distributed through the Midland and Western Districts, though in unequal proportions, as the Midland contained far more than the Western. In some of its counties (the Midland) there was not a single known Catholic." The same writer gives the number of chapels for the Midland District as " about fifty," and only thirty secular clergy; and " some of the chapels were without pastors ". This will be quite apparent, as the priests were fewer by twenty than the chapels; though, as a matter of fact, of which we have evidence in our own time, many of the clergy would serve more than one chapel. According to the Government statistics, to be quoted in full later on, there were, before the year 1801, one hundred and fifty-six chapels in England and Wales " erected or appropriated to religious use ".

---

[1] Payne's *Old English Catholic Missions*. [2] Husenbeth's *Life of Milner*.

Previous to the year 1824, no official Catholic list of the number of Catholic chapels was published, but from that year the number was stated in the annual *Directory*. In 1824, there were in England and Wales 346 churches and chapels, and of that number 5 were in Wales. In 1829, the year of emancipation, there were in England 389, in Wales 6 churches and chapels. In 1840, the number stood, England 457, Wales 6, showing an increase of 124 churches and chapels.

Before the year 1839, there does not appear to have existed any authentic record as to the number of priests, but in that year the number is given as 536, and in the following year 542.

From the year 1824, the Catholic Church began to make steady progress, and that progress seemed even fifty years ago to have created alarm in the minds of some non-Catholics. In a review [1] published in 1839, there is an article on "The Present State of the Catholic Controversy," in which occurs the following passage: "That there is an increase of Catholics in England, and an increase calling imperatively for some counteracting effect, may be safely believed". The same article pointed out as an argument for increased watchfulness that there were at that time in England and Wales 446 Catholic churches and chapels. What line the "counteracting effect" should take the article did not discuss.

In 1838, there were only 197 places registered for the celebration of marriages in Catholic chapels, and for this privilege a tax of three pounds per chapel was levied. Although the progress of the Catholic religion between 1824 and 1840 was considerable, it was not effected without many difficulties. In 1833, one of the Catholic bishops in his pastoral lamented that the clergy "had to roam over the country for weeks and months in search of means to erect a house, a school, a chapel".[2]

The following table not only gives the actual number of churches, but exhibits the increase, and apportions the same to the various counties. Compared with recent statistics, these results appear small indeed, but considering that the Church had barely emerged from the dark shadow under which she had so long lain, they afford another instance of her marvellous vitality.

The totals of this table show for the seventeen years it covers a net increase (deducting the decrease of seven) of 117 churches and chapels.

---

[1] *Eclectic Review*.   [2] *The Lamp*, Nov. 18, 1865.

Statistics as to Number and Increase of Catholic Churches and Chapels between 1824 and 1840.[1]

COUNTIES.	1824.	1832.	1840.	INCREASE.	DECREASE.
Bedford	...	1	1	1	...
Berks	5	6	6	1	...
Bucks	1	1	1	...	...
Cambridge	1	2	1	...	...
Cheshire	5	7	10	5	...
Cornwall	2	2	2	...	...
Cumberland	4	5	7	3	2
Derby	7	8	9	2	...
Devon	6	9	9	3	...
Dorset	7	7	9	2	...
Durham	12	13	17	5	...
Essex	5	7	7	2	...
Gloucester	5	7	8	3	...
Hampshire	12	15	12	...	...
Hereford	2	4	4	2	...
Hertford	...	1	1	1	...
Kent	7	8	10	3	...
Lancashire	80	84	89	9	...
Leicester	7	6	12	5	...
Lincoln	11	10	10	...	1
Middlesex	17	19	20	3	...
Monmouth	...	6	8	8	...
Norfolk	9	8	7	...	...
Northampton	1	1	5	4	...
Northumberland	10	18	19	9	...
Notts	5	3	3	...	2
Oxford	9	7	7	...	2
Salop	5	7	9	4	...
Somerset	7	8	12	5	...
Stafford	17	25	32	15	...
Suffolk	6	5	6	...	...
Surrey	5	5	7	2	...
Sussex	6	6	7	1	...
Warwick	8	13	19	11	...
Westmoreland	2	2	2	...	...
Wilts	3	3	3	...	...
Worcester	7	9	12	5	...
Yorks	45	48	54	9	...
WALES.					
Brecknock	1	1	1	...	...
Carnarvon	1	1	1	...	...
Denbigh	1	1	1	...	...
Glamorgan	1	1	1	...	...
Flint	1	2	2	1	...
Totals	346	402	463	124	7

[1] Compiled from "Catholic Statistics, 1823 to 1853". London and Derby: Richardson, 1853.

Supplementary to these figures may be given the Government returns of the year 1851, from which it appears that the Catholic body had the following churches and chapels " erected or appropriated to religious use in England and Wales ".

Before 1801, 156; from 1801 to 1811, 28; 1811 to 1821, 29; 1821 to 1831, 52; 1831 to 1841, 92—total, 357.

Statistics showing the Position of the Catholic Religion in England and Wales with respect to Priests and Churches from 1841 to 1850.

District.	1841.		1845.		1850.		Increase.	
	Priests.	Churches.	Priests.	Churches.	Priests.	Churches.	Priests.	Churches.
London	106	73	133	84	168	104	62	31
Central	110	106	122	106	165	117	55	11
Eastern	31	33	34	35	40	38	9	5
Western	54	40	68	45	70	59	16	19
Lancashire . . .	124	97	166	112	187	130	63	33
Yorkshire . . .	59	55	65	59	66	61	7	6
Northern . . .	54	46	58	51	67	51	13	5
Welsh	19	19	20	16	25	21	6	2
Totals	557	469	666	508	788	581	231	112

NOTE.—In the census returns of 1851 (" Religious Worship in England and Wales ") the number of Catholic churches and chapels "erected or appropriated to religious use in England and Wales " for the decade 1841-1851 is given as 92.

From this statement it will be noticeable that the largest increase is shown in the London, Lancashire, and Central Districts. In the other districts the progress (if any) was of a very feeble character. The first-named district of course at the outset contained the largest number of Catholics. Lancashire has always maintained the reputation of being the most Catholic county in England, and the Central District included Staffordshire, also a county containing all through the Catholic persecution period a considerable number of English Catholics.

Of all the unjust laws suffered by the Catholics of this country there was none perhaps which bore more heavily upon them than the marriage laws. The iniquity of making the marriage of a

Catholic by a priest a penal act, or a non-valid act, was a thing which to-day we may comprehend in all its fulness. The non-possession of the franchise, or the enforced payment of the double land tax, were matters affecting the civil status of the Catholic body; but the prevention of priests from exercising their spiritual functions was a direct interference with the liberty of the subject. The Catholic may have been permitted to receive the sacrament of matrimony in private or in public, but the law did not take cognisance of such marriage, and by a peculiar legal aspect the offspring of such marriage were "illegitimate". The legislators did not consider the pain and humiliation which Catholics must have felt at being compelled to be united in matrimony by the clergy of the Protestant Church. There was of course no Catholic ecclesiastical penalty attached to such service, it being the "law of the land" and on a par with the reading of the burial service, and was perforce permitted and submitted to. But there were frequent protests, as in 1823 the Right Rev. Dr. Poynter called attention to the marriage laws in a petition to Parliament praying that the Roman Catholics in England might be put on the same footing as those in Ireland in this respect. In connection with this subject Sir James Mackintosh referred to the petition of parish officers of a large and populous district, complaining of the burden brought upon them and the injury to the country generally in consequence of the law making the marriage of the Catholics by their own clergymen unlawful. On this occasion a complaint was made against the Catholic clergy by a Mr. Taylor, M.P., and the expression made use of by that gentleman will illustrate the position of English Catholics, both clergy and laity, in 1823. This member stated that many of the inconveniences complained of might be attributed to the conduct of Catholic priests themselves, for "they must know such marriages [that of Catholics by their own clergy] were null and void, and they (the Catholic clergy) ought therefore to refuse to perform the ceremony until the parties had been married according to the rites of the Church of England ".[1]

Notwithstanding these endeavours the laws affecting marriage remained in force for several years after this attempt at their amendment.

---

[1] Quoted in Madden's *Penal Laws* from *Parliamentary Debates*, new series, pp. 965, 966, 967.

Table showing the Position of the Catholic Church in this Country with respect to Elementary Education up to the year 1851, with a comparison as to the relative educational status of the most numerous of the non-Catholic sects.[1]

ENGLAND and WALES—Dates at which Existing Schools were established.

DESCRIPTION OF SCHOOLS. DENOMINATIONAL—Class III.	No. of Existing Schools.	Before 1801.	1801 to 1811.	1811 to 1821.	1821 to 1831.	1831 to 1841.	1841 to 1851.	Date not Specified.	In each of the last Ten Years.											Three Months 1851.
									1841.	1842.	1843.	1844.	1845.	1846.	1847.	1848.	1849.	1850.	
Independents, British	183	3	3	6	5	43	116	7	12	1	4	17	21	16	16	5	9	11	4
,, Others	248	5	6	6	16	52	153	10	6	6	10	19	21	19	23	14	13	16	6
Baptists, British	51	2	1	4	6	6	35	3	1	3	4	2	8	5	3	4	1	1	1
,, Others	64	2	2	1	4	12	43	...	2	1	3	5	4	4	6	3	7	6	2
Society of Friends, British	5	...	...	1	...	3	...	1	...	...	...	...	...	...	...	...	...	...	...
,, Others	18	...	...	3	4	3	8	...	...	...	...	...	...	...	...	...	...	...	...
Unitarians, British	4	1	...	...	3	...	...	1	...	...	...	...	...	...	...	...	...	...	...
,, Others	26	7	1	1	1	3	13	1	...	...	1	4	1	1	4	1	2	1	...
Wesleyan Methodists, British	20	1	...	1	1	6	6	5	...	...	...	...	1	...	1	...	1	...	...
,, Others	343	6	4	16	16	56	233	12	10	8	13	27	48	28	29	19	20	26	5
Methodist, New Connection, British	3	...	...	...	...	1	...	1	...	...	...	...	...	...	...	...	1	...	...
,, Others	10	...	1	1	...	...	7	1	...	...	...	1	...	...	...	...	1	...	...
Primitive Methodists, British	2	...	...	...	1	1	...	...	...	...	...	...	...	...	...	...	...	...	...
,, Others	23	...	...	1	...	3	16	2	1	...	...	2	...	1	4	5	1	3	4
Wesleyan Methodist Association	10	...	...	...	...	2	7	1	...	...	...	...	...	3	1	1	2	1	...
Calvinistic Methodists, British	22	...	...	...	...	...	22	...	...	2	...	1	4	5	3	1	3	6	...
,, Others	19	1	...	...	3	4	11	...	...	...	1	2	1	4	2	1	2	2	1
Dissenters (not defined), British	28	...	...	3	...	10	15	...	...	1	2	2	1	1	1	1	4	1	1
,, Others	15	2	2	2	2	2	5	...	...	1	...	2	1	...	2	...	...	...	3
Catholics	**311**	**10**	**10**	**14**	**28**	**69**	**166**	**14**	**7**	**9**	**8**	**8**	**18**	**6**	**17**	**20**	**21**	**44**	**3**

[1] Compiled from the Education Census of 1851.

CHAPTER XIII.

THE ATTITUDE OF THE CATHOLIC CHURCH IN ENGLAND AND WALES ON EDUCATION—1800-1870.

A DISTINGUISHED convert to the Catholic faith, in writing of the poetry of the Church, has made use of these words: " Such poets as are born under her shadow she takes into her service ; . . . nay, she can even make schoolmen of them, as she made of St. Thomas, till logic becomes poetical ".[1]

Nothing more historically true could be expressed of the attitude of the Universal Church with regard to education. She has ever been the patron of learning. In the olden times much of the possessions of the wealthy went to the founding and endowment of schools. The Church was education itself, education was part of her system, and upon her fell the responsibility of seeing that the people were taught. She did a noble work in this respect, and if she did not accomplish more it certainly was not due to her remissness. The Church has always recognised the principle that the State exists for the people ; not the people for the State. She has distinguished between things temporal and things spiritual, and in so doing has always taught that education to be full and entire must have its basis on a Christian groundwork—in other words, that religion must occupy a first place. Hence the formation of colleges, seminaries, catechetical classes. It was under the Church's direction that the monks translated the pages of Holy Writ before the invention of printing. To her the world is indebted for the preservation of the Scriptures.

At the Reformation the light which the Church had shed was temporarily extinguished, and the propagators of the new religion did not concern themselves as to the education of the people. Of the reformed religion the people seemed to know nothing, save that non-compliance therewith would subject them to persecution. There was robbery on a gigantic scale, and funds intended to assist in the education of the people were soon appropriated for base and unworthy purposes. This being so, it is no wonder that at the beginning of the present century the people of England were in a state of degradation and ignorance. That such was the case

---

[1] Article on the " Christian Year," in *Essays, Critical and Historical*, by J. H. Newman, vol. ii. p. 441.

is no figure of speech nor statement made for contrast between that time and the preceding periods when the education of the people was a matter of concern to the Church. Formerly education was not a State function, but a function which the Church took upon herself. That at the commencement of this century the people were ignorant can be proved, and in the dry, hard words of the Government reports, leaving aside the writers of history, who are all agreed upon the point. "The records and recollections to be obtained of society at the beginning of the century," we are told, " bear testimony to a state of ignorance and immorality so dense, and general, that if any member of the present generation could be suddenly transported to that earlier period he would scarcely be able to believe himself in England."[1] Such is the admitted state of affairs, such the results of the work accomplished at the end of two hundred and seventy years from the inauguration of the "Glorious Reformation". The first year of the nineteenth century marked a period of 112 years from another "glorious" period, the Revolution, the *annus mirabilis*, a year wonderful indeed, but in the inverse sense in which the expression is frequently accepted, for it was the precursor of more than a century of darkness for the people, and heralded a time of general and dense ignorance and immorality. England had produced many learned men between the time of the Revolution and the early years of the present century, but *the people*[2] were neglected, and the results of the Reformation and the manner in which the

---

[1] Education Census, 1851.

[2] The genius of Dryden appears to have had little effect on the Protestant British mind. The age of Newton was also the age of Swift and Bolingbroke, who were both sceptics and the forerunners (may it be said, tutors?) of Voltaire and of the French Revolution—in other words, of the far-spreading infidelity of the modern world. The stupendous genius of Swift, his awful invective and his colossal blasphemy, have probably been never equalled by any other writer of prose. Montesquieu, who was much in London, imbibed a great deal of the fashionable Deism, which, having been propagated by the French Revolution, has now become Agnosticism, or, in other words, mere Atheism. There can be little doubt but the British Empire owes the large fragments of Christianity it still possesses to two wonderful men, Johnson and Cowper. They both led lives of prayer—their writings had enormous influence on the thinkers who inaugurated the nineteenth century. Cowper died in 1800, twenty-two years after Voltaire, of whom he wrote:—

"The Bible was his jest-book whence he drew
Bon mots to vex the Christian and the Jew".

new Church attended to the educational wants of the people is forcibly exhibited in the above quotation. We are bound, however, in justice to state that, however remiss the Church of England may have been up to the year 1800, for the first twenty years of the present century such educational work as was accomplished was due in a great measure to her efforts, and that she thereby retrieved much of the stigma connected with her attitude prior to that time. The year 1818 seems to have been the first year in which the English Government exhibited any inclination to study the educational requirements of the people. A return ordered by Parliament showed that one in seventeen of the population were receiving some kind of elementary education ; and fifteen years later (1833) one in eleven of the population were being instructed. There was begun in 1834 " a system of national education by a small annual grant towards the erection of schools, and developed in 1839 by the creation of a committee of the Privy Council for educational purposes, and by the steady increase of educational grants ".[1] The state of " education " in England little over half-a-century ago was shown in a speech on the Education Bill of 1847 by Mr. Macaulay, in which he stated : " You will find that 130,000 couples were married in 1844. More than 50,000 bridegrooms and 60,000 of the brides did not sign their names, but made their mark."[2] As before stated, no defined action was taken by any Government until 1833, but in that year and the following six years the sum of £20,000 was annually allowed for education purposes. The whole of this money was paid to Protestant societies—the Catholic body got not one penny. Before the year 1847 no grants were made except to assist in building schools, and the cost of education was borne by voluntary bodies. Of the half-million of Government money paid for schools between 1839 and 1850 the sum for the Catholic body amounted exactly to £1049.[3]

Notwithstanding these large grants, there were in 1851 no

---

[1] Green's *Short History of English People*.

[2] Macaulay, Speech on Education, 1847.

[3] " The total amount of public money granted from 1833 to the end of 1850 was, as nearly as possible, £1,000,000. Of the £500,000 spent between 1839-50 upon English schools, £405,000 was contributed to schools connected with the Established Church, the other denominations receiving—Wesleyans £8000, and Catholics £1049. The British and Foreign School Society received £51,000."—Census 1851—Education, p. xviii. The sum therefore represented the " share " allotted to Catholics up to the year 1850.

fewer than 3,663,261 children with respect to whom there was "apparently no reason other than the parents' pleasure they should not be at school".[1]

What, meanwhile, had been the attitude of the Catholics on education for the first half of this century? And, in considering this, it must be remembered that for the first thirty years of this century the Catholics were not considered worthy of civil rights, and their condition was one that did not permit of rapid progress. In the year 1820 in some of the English counties there was not a single Catholic church or chapel. In 1833 when the Government began to bestir itself there were in England three counties with only one church each, four counties with two churches, and two counties with three each—that is, in nine counties only fourteen churches. From this condition of affairs it could scarcely be expected that there should be anything like a proportion between schools and churches. A priest may have more than one church to attend to, but a schoolmaster is of necessity a stationary being; and the maintenance of a school was and is frequently more costly than that of a church. At that time there was no systematic training, and from this we shall best comprehend the difficulties that lay in the way. The Catholic body had from time to time made such efforts as they could in the direction of elementary education. We read, for instance, that on April 29, 1824, a meeting of the East End Catholic Association was held, with the Hon. Edward Petre in the chair. An appeal had been issued by the society, which stated that "the liberal manner in which the appeal of the East End Catholic Association was met by the public in the year 1821 greatly aided in the establishment of schools for the education of poor children of both sexes upon a more extended system than had before been attempted in the eastern part of the metropolis". Bishop Challoner strongly exerted himself in the matter of education. In a biographical account of that great prelate[2] we are told that "Dr. Challoner instituted a school for girls at Hammersmith, and one for boys at Wolverhampton," and that he "particularly protected the *Education Society*, now [1824] the chief branch of the Associated Catholic Charities".

The attitude of the Church on education has always been the same, because of her fixed and unchangeable principles and teachings. In May, 1840, was held the "annual dinner of

---

[1] Education Census, 1851.   [2] *Catholic Spectator*, 1824.

the Associated Catholic Charities," the Hon. Edward Petre in the chair. He was supported by Lords Clifford and Camoys, and a great number of the Catholic gentry were present. The honorable Chairman, in the course of a speech, said that none were more taxed than the Catholics; and yet they got none of the grants for education; they paid much, but received nothing. They were told that it was not for them the grant was intended. Hence they were driven to their own resources; and, he must confess, he did not regret it. Catholics had been driven to their own resources before. And what had they done? He pointed for the answer to the colleges they had founded abroad in times when education was prohibited; and he pointed also to the chapels which they had erected at home. He would not now refer to the immense funds set aside for education by the Catholics, and which funds he had always declared, and would ever declare, had been unjustly wrenched from them.

In responding to the toast of "The Catholic Peers of the Realm," Lord Clifford said a few years ago he and his Catholic brethren of the peerage could not have referred to their conduct in Parliament; and now they could do so, he was proud to say that they had not allied themselves with the majority in the House of Lords. He was glad that the Catholic peers had been admitted into Parliament, because they had shown themselves the friends of civil and religious liberty. So long as they did so he was proud to belong to them, but no longer. When the address to the Queen against the Education Grant was taken up, he was delighted to say that not one Catholic peer joined in it. He felt that the Catholic peers could not better serve the throne than by laboring to educate the people upon principles of religion and virtue; and no measure of education which excluded the Catholics would be a measure of justice.

From the Government census on education we gather that in 1850 or thereabout in addition to the efforts of the Church of England " most of the other religious bodies have also established day schools, more or less; the Roman Catholics especially ".

This will be seen by referring to the table (p. 66), as in the decade 1841-51 no fewer than 166 schools were established by the Catholic body. The Catholics did not receive consideration without having experienced many obstacles, and even the members of the Government had misgivings as to the payment of public funds towards the education of Catholic children. In the debate in the House of Commons, April 19, 1847, Lord John Russell said: " It has been asked if Roman Catholics are to be included. To that I answer that in the minutes of December, 1846, the question was not entered into. Then the question came if a desire were expressed by the Roman Catholics to have schools for Catholics and Catholics only I would be in favor of it, but the greatest care should be taken in dealing with this subject, and I think, for example, that it would not do to support monastic schools for the education of Roman Catholics." His Lordship also believed it would " hardly be expedient to expend any of the £100,000 in aid of Roman Catholic schools," and, he continued, " I believe that of all the half-million which has been already spent under the direction of the Treasury *not one shilling* was given in aid of the Roman Catholic schools ". On the same evening Lord Brougham presented a petition and expressed surprise that the recent application for aid for Roman Catholic schools should have met with the answer that the question should be " considered ". They all knew that in England there were few Roman Catholic schools, and he expressed surprise that the great question of Education should have been mixed up with all the broiling of sectarian violence. At this stage, according to our authority, " the Roman Catholic children were finally excluded from any participation of the £100,000 that formed part of the Government scheme of education ! "[1] On May 25, 1849, the views of the Catholic body on education were clearly defined in a letter written by the Poor School Committee to the Committee of Council on Education, in these words : " The Roman Catholic Church claims for her clergy the sole and exclusive charge of the religious and moral training of her children and a power to frame the regulations connected therewith ".[2]

In the "general report" on Roman Catholic schools for 1849 the inspector wrote : " No one, however, who recognises the office of the ministers of religion as the natural guardians and instructors of the children of the poor can blame the jealous solicitude with which they acquit themselves of their special responsibilities," and in support of this the inspector quoted a recent observation of the Duc de Broglie that " wherever *liberty of conscience* is included in the catalogue of constitutional principles, there *liberty of instruction* must exist together with it, both by strict justice and wise policy". Further, if any proof were needed of the principle already

---

[1] Madden's *Penal Laws against Roman Catholics*.
[2] Minutes and Correspondence of Committee of Council on Education, 1848-9.

alluded to, that education to be thorough must have a religious groundwork, we read in the same report: " It was impossible to pass through these schools [the Roman Catholic schools] without being forced, as it were, to observe the fact that the religious spirit controls and penetrates them in every direction. '. . . It is evident that the managers of these schools do not conceive education to consist in the development of particular faculties to the neglect of others . . . but that they justly regard it as the training of the whole man for the fulfilment of the destinies which await him both in this world and the next." The writer further testified that he had seen " practised ingenuity exhaust itself in proposing the most difficult and delicate questions in Christian doctrine and Bible history, without once succeeding in baffling the knowledge of those who were interrogated," and, he added, " I have witnessed this so often that I am obliged to consider it the main characteristic, as it is certainly the special charm and praise of the schools in question ". These words were written at a time when public elementary education was in its infancy, at the time the Government of the country had awakened to the fact that ignorance prevailed throughout the country to an alarming extent. What, it may be asked, was the prevailing notion of liberty of conscience in Catholic schools? Let the express terms of the inspector again be quoted in answer to this. " The universal rule is, for I have not met with a single exception, that in no case do the children receive religious instruction without the express sanction or request of their parents, and that either they are at liberty to absent themselves from the school altogether when it is communicated or else the Catholic children are withdrawn to some convenient place, commonly to the church or chapel, in order to be instructed apart. The just susceptibility of religious prepossessions is thus duly consulted and respected, and they who demand liberty of conscience as their own most cherished right are careful to avoid the criminal inconsistency of violating that sacred privilege in their dealings with others."[1]

[1] Minutes of Committee of Council on Education, 1848-9-50, vol. ii. p. 520.

The Government of the period 1840-50 was extremely niggardly in grants to Catholic schools. The population of England and Wales in 1851 was 17,927,609. In the Census Report on Religious Worship in England and Wales the number of attendants on Census Sunday at Catholic places of worship was 395,303. Commenting on this, the Census Report for Education, p. lxii., states: " The total number of persons of this (the Catholic) faith cannot be less than

To an outsider, as well as to the Catholic student of history, the thought may suggest itself, how is it that the poorest and smallest of the sects had at the commencement of the century the largest number of schools ? The reply to this would be that the Church in supplying schools was simply carrying out her traditions, and an examination of these figures will prove the earnest desire of the Catholics to establish schools. The Wesleyans, it will be seen, had only seven schools established before 1801 and the Catholics ten. Yet the Wesleyan body was formed out of a rich church. In the race the Catholics were ahead until 1841. The Wesleyan body had meanwhile been growing rapidly in volume, and that they were no small sect even at the beginning of the century is apparent from the fact that many of their chapels still remaining were built in the two last decades of the eighteenth century. It will also be easy to establish that the Catholics were compared to the Wesleyans and many other sects, a much poorer body, both in numbers and in worldly possessions. In March, 1851, the great Wesleyan body had only fifty-two schools ahead of the Catholics, and a glance at the figures will show that the latter in a comparative sense exceeded in educational efforts all other sects. The history of the Catholic Church as regards education up to 1851 is a point to be regarded by the Catholics with pride. The struggles, the adversities, and the ultimate triumphs culminating in the period we are now dealing with resulted in the laying of a foundation whereby it has been found possible to train up a new generation of Catholics.

Haydock and Lingard died at this epoch (1850-51). These two scholars did much to dispel the ignorant prejudices of the age. Father Haydock, who was an accomplished scholar, belonged to an ancient Catholic family of Cottam Hall, near Preston. His great work, viz., a new edition of the Douai Bible, first published by the English College at Douai A.D. 1609, and the New Testament, first published at Rheims 1582, appeared in three folio volumes printed at Manchester in 1811. Haydock's Catholic Bible is too well known to need comment; suffice it to say that it is a work of great theological and literary erudition.

1,000,000, and probably exceeds that number ". Whilst, roughly speaking, the Catholic body represented one in 18 of the population, they received for education as though they were one in 485. Among educational bodies they occupied the honorable position of *fourth* on the list, whilst relatively their position would have been *eighteenth*. This speaks well for the noble efforts made for the education of Catholic children. The Wesleyan body had 381 schools, with 41,144 scholars; the Catholics 339 and 41,382 scholars. The Wesleyans, however, with fewer scholars received £8000 against £1049 allowed to the Catholic body between 1839-50.

In the year 1857 there was an important expression of opinion on religious education by the late Cardinal Wiseman. His Eminence in an address on education spoke as follows: "It is impossible to train up a child as he should be trained, and not to bring him up in the love of God. . . . Thus let us teach the science of God, binding and combining everything in nature with His love."[1]

The inspector for the Southern Division of England wrote, in 1859, of the remarkable progress of schools for the Catholic poor in London, and also stated that great and successful exertions had been made which, perhaps, surpassed anything which he had witnessed in any part of England. The number of separate institutions visited by him annually in London and the suburbs for March, 1859, was 64: and the number of departments, including industrial and night schools, was 121. Of the efforts of the Religious the inspector wrote: "Several other schools, taught also by members of religious communities, and especially the ladies who founded the college at St. Leonards, deserve particular mention. The schools of the Sisters of Mercy at Chelsea, St. Joseph's, and Moorfields are also taught with much ability, while those at Charles Street, and Brompton, under the Sisters of Compassion, are of a kind which I can hardly venture to praise: in the presence of such astonishing labor and devotion, one can only maintain a respectful silence." The same year the inspector for the North-Western Division (the late Mr. S. N. Stokes) wrote: "Schools are multiplied; buildings are better planned and furnished; more suitable accommodation provided for children of tender age; trained teachers find employment in greater numbers; discipline and instruction are of a higher order". Staffordshire alone presented a retrograde aspect, and a law dispute had one effect, as the disputed possession of the Shrewsbury estates had "led to the removal of certificated teachers from Alton and Cheadle". In the North-Western District the teachers had increased in one year from 112 to 129. The inspector for the North of England reported a "serious grievance". Proselytism was at work in his district, as "many Protestant mill-owners obliged the parents of Catholic children in their mills to pay school pence to their Protestant school mills". This system was in striking contrast to the Catholic interpretation

---

[1] Cardinal Wiseman on "Religious Education". *The Lamp*, June 6, 1857.

of liberty of conscience as referred to in a preceding quotation of the words of Her Majesty's inspector. But the Catholic parents were steadfast. There was a double tax, as the inspector pointed out that "as the parents are poor, they cannot afford to pay again for their children's schooling in Catholic schools; and as they are conscientious they cannot agree to their children risking the salvation of their souls, by mixing with other children who are frequently of immoral habits, and who mock at their faith. Thus placed, many of these children receive no instructing save that of their Sunday school." In 1864, the Government reports showed still further progress in elementary education. Between 1854 and 1864 the number of masters trained at Hammersmith was 137, and the Liverpool College from 1856 to 1864 had sent out 22 trained mistresses. The following are the statistics for 1864, and they may be read in connection with the particulars for 1890, thus giving in detail educational progress during 26 years. In 1864, there were in England and Wales 215 schools, with accommodation for 60,058 children. Present at examination, 40,283. The voluntary contributions for the year amounted to £11,292; school pence, £9500; and the grant earned from Government was £4424. In the year 1870, the Government inspector for the North-Western Division of England, comprising Lancashire, Cheshire, Salop, and North Wales, dealing with Catholic education in these counties, wrote: "Numerically the progress of schools has been great in methods of teaching, and results of instruction greater still. In 1853, only 28 schools were in receipt of annual grants from the Committee of Council. In 1853, no facilities existed for training teachers. In 1870, there had been flourishing for several years a training college for school-mistresses, which more than anything else promoted the growth of elementary education amongst the Roman Catholics of Great Britain." The report went on to say: "In 1853, Manchester and Salford scarcely showed any satisfactory results of education, but now enjoy the advantage of many excellent schools. On the whole the number of aided schools was multiplied fivefold, and the increase never stopped."

This report may be regarded as typical of the progress of Catholic education throughout England and Wales between the years 1847 and 1870.

CHAPTER XIV.

THE ANGLICAN MOVEMENT.[1]

In that part of the history of our own times which immediately concerns the Catholic Church there is one movement which more than any other has an important bearing on the position of the Church in this country.

Need we say that this was and is the great Anglican movement—a movement which has affected the Church's history even more than the restoration of the hierarchy? In the records of modern history there are periods or movements which demand more than ordinary comment at the hands of the historian. These movements, or political and religious eras, may be roughly summarised as those relating to electoral reform, the corn laws, the commencement of primary education under Government control in 1847, the Education Act of 1870, with its additions and experiments, and many other matters. During the past half-century noble and liberal laws have been passed affecting the requirements of the people—such, for instance, as those in connection with the housing of the poor, and the occupations of the working classes whether in the mine, the factory, or workshop. Attempts have been made to adjust the relations between capital and labour, and a Royal Commission has recently been appointed to inquire into the labor question. The franchise, too, has been developed, almost to the extent of manhood suffrage. What, it may be asked, have these matters to do with the history of the Catholic Church? The answer to such a question is that, placed side by side with the great movement we are now considering, their results would appear to be far less reaching upon the contemporary history of England. The movements we have alluded to caused great upheavals; but no portion of modern history has created the revolution and called for comment equal to that which the " Tracts for the Times " called forth. For half-a-century it has agitated the English-speaking people, and still its effects are visible. The movement is one of all the tenses—it refers to the past, it affects

---

[1] " The Catholic Church . . . saw the commencement of all the Governments and of all the Ecclesiastical establishments that now exist in the world ; and we feel no assurance that she is not destined to see the end of them all."— Macaulay's Essay on *Ranke's History of the Popes.*

the present; and as to the future, its full effect must be gauged by another generation. When the history of the nineteenth century is written, this movement must, of necessity, claim a large share of consideration from the writers of history. Yet the movement was not a Catholic one, but exclusively Protestant; and the most bigoted anti-Catholic cannot ascribe it in any way to the Catholic Church.

Briefly considered, what was the Tractarian movement? It was a movement on the part of some zealous and distinguished members of the Church of England to discover in that Church either the Catholic Church itself, or a branch thereof. They sought to discover and develop the " continuity " theory—in other words, that the Church of England was similar in character to that founded by Christ.

As the " Tracts " proceeded the more " unorthodox " became their tone so far as that term is understood outside the Catholic Church. The attitude of the writers may be compared to that of the humble student of science, who, debarred of regular training, arrives intuitively at scientific truth. They resembled the Pagan philosophers of old, who, working in darkness and without the help of revealed religion, yet propounded truths approaching to those of Christianity itself. Still it was an honest movement, and the writers knew not whither they were drifting. They were as mariners tossed about by the billows, yet withal destined to be directed by God into the haven of rest. They started on their work not with love for the Catholic Church but rather with bitterness towards her. Only nine years before the reception of the greatest of the Tractarians into the Church, John Henry Newman wrote of her: " Let it be considered whether there be not some peculiarities hanging about her which are sufficient from prudential motives to keep us at a distance from her ".[1] Still Dr. Newman in spite of this utterance lamented the want of unity in the Anglican Church even amongst the clergy; and of the laity he wrote: " Much less do the laity receive that instruction in one and the same doctrine, which is the evidence as may be fairly alleged of their being taught of the Lord. They wander about like sheep without a shepherd; they do not know what to believe, and are thrown on their private judgment, weak and inadequate as it is,

---

[1] " Lectures on the Prophetical Offices of the Church, by John Henry Newman, B.D., Fellow of Oriel College and Vicar of St. Mary the Virgin's, Oxford," 1837.

merely because they do not know whither to betake themselves for guidance."

How prophetic these words, and how little did the writer at that time look upon himself as a lost sheep! In the way of Divine Providence it fell out that this distinguished man was destined to be "taught of the Lord," to be one of the fold under the Good Shepherd, to know what to believe, to place reliance not on private judgment, but on the unerring teaching of God's Church, and finally to be one who by the depth of his piety and the greatness of his learning should shed lustre even on the Sacred College of the Holy Roman Church.[1]

Still the "Tracts" were proceeded with. The Thirty-nine Articles or some of them were commented on in a manner which gave rise to alarm and consternation.

At length came the climax. "Tract XC." was more than the orthodox Bishop of Oxford could tolerate, and it was formally condemned.[2] Meanwhile the work had borne fruit, and receptions into the Church were numerous. On 8th October, 1845, the author of the tract wrote to a friend: "I am this night expecting Father Dominic the Passionist. . . . He does not know of my intention, but I mean to ask of him admission into the One Fold of Christ."

What has been the result of the movement so far as can be gauged at the present day? One of the chief results is that great numbers have been received into the Catholic Church.[3]

The secession of Dr. Newman,[4] wrote the Earl of Beaconsfield, "dealt a blow to the Church of England, under which she still reels". Another great statesman (Mr. Gladstone), representing an opposite school of political thought, wrote five years later

[1] See letter of Leo XIII. to the Cardinal Archbishop of Westminster on the death of Cardinal Newman.

[2] For a full account of the agitation caused by this tract, see Cardinal Newman's *Apologia* and Dean Stanley's *Essays*.

[3] In a "History of the Tractarian Movement," written in 1856 by a converted Anglican clergyman (Edward George Kirwan Brown), there is in his *Tractarian Harvest* a list of over 200 Anglican clergymen besides a great number of distinguished laity who between 1842 and 1856 joined the Catholic Church. Alzog's *Manual of Universal Church History*, vol. iv. p. 264 (Dublin: Gill, 1885), states that in 1867 the number of distinguished converts to the Catholic Church in England was 867, of whom 243 had been Anglican ministers. From the same work we learn that in 1851 33 of the Anglican clergy, including the then Archdeacon Manning, joined the Church.

[4] Preface to Disraeli's *Works*, 1870.

that "nothing more calamitous had occurred to the Church of England since the partial secession of John Wesley than had the secession of Dr. Newman".[1]

But the movement did more than take away Newman from the English Church. It denuded her of men of intellect and culture—men who half-a-century ago were the hope of that Church. True, Keble and Pusey remained Tractarians. Of the former, his contemporary wrote that to the Anglican Church he was its "renovator, so far as it has been renovated".[2]

The latter, though he did not follow in the steps of many of his brethren, may be regarded as the father of Ritualism: a movement which has done much within our own time to place the Catholic Church in a new light before the people of England. In many other ways is the work of Tractarianism visible. It has caused to be taught in the Church of England Catholic doctrines, Catholic hymns are used, the works of the saints are quoted by the clergy, and recommended for spiritual reading. The holy days of the year are observed. The principle of fasting is inculcated, and confession is openly advocated.

Has this great movement affected the people at large, or has it not? We must acknowledge that so far it has rather borne fruit among the learned and the wealthy. What we have to consider is whether the Anglican movement may be regarded as an *unmitigated* good. There is always an alternative view of examining these questions, and it must be admitted that whilst the movement brought into the Church many great men, it has developed other tendencies. Doctrines which fifty years ago would have been considered unorthodox are now tolerated. The Church of England boldly proclaims that she is Catholic, and that the views recently adopted have always been held. She professes to distinguish between "Catholic" and "Roman Catholic," and the new generation are being taught many Catholic truths as though these were part of the inheritance of the Church of England. The position taken up is untenable, but it is put in force, and this we may regard as one of the unforeseen conditions arising from the movement we now treat of. The generality of people have neither time, ability, nor opportunities for solving for themselves abstruse

---

[1] See quotation on *Vaticanism*.

[2] See Essay on the "Christian Year" in Dr. Newman's *Essays, Historical and Critical*, vol. ii. p. 441.

points. This is a matter which may well deserve the attention of the heads of the Church in England, though of late years a society[1] has done much to disseminate information on controversial questions by explaining away the many fallacies connected with the new Anglican departure. But we may reasonably conclude that on the whole the Anglican movement has been of great use to the Church, for if it had accomplished nothing else, it has tended to soften asperities, and to lessen prejudices, and, above all, it has given to the people of England part of the Truth of which the Catholic Church alone is the custodian for the benefit of mankind. It is not, therefore, unreasonable to hope that the propagation of Catholic doctrines may lead to another great harvest in the submission of numbers of the English people to the Church of their fathers.

CHAPTER XV.

THE RESTORATION OF THE HIERARCHY IN ENGLAND.

"WE were the Roman Catholics, not a sect, not even an interest as men conceived it—not a body, however small, representative of the great communion abroad—but a mere handful of individuals who might be counted like the pebbles and detritus of the great deluge, and who, forsooth, merely happened to retain a creed which in its day indeed was the profession of a Church."—Dr. Newman, *The Second Spring* (1852.)

The history of the Catholic Church in England since the time of James II. presents many phases and many epochs. Much of that history is painful to contemplate, chronicling as it does the sufferings endured by our Catholic forefathers for the faith. It is the history of cruelty, persecution, robbery, and endurance. A Church alien to the people robbed the Catholics of their beautiful cathedrals and churches, and to crown the injustice, the titles of the ancient sees were usurped at the will of despotic monarchs, and in place of the bishops of the orthodox Church of England were placed men whose only title (if title it may be called) was the favorable notice of such as were at the head of temporal affairs, or those with favor at the Court. A spiritual Church in direct communion with the Holy See was suppressed, in order

---

[1] Catholic Truth Society.

that the creatures of monarchs should profess to exercise spiritual jurisdiction.

The ancient hierarchy of England became extinct September 27, 1584, by the death of Dr. Thomas Watson, Bishop of Lincoln. Between that date and March 23, 1623, a period of thirty-nine years, the Catholics were as a flock without shepherds; but in the last-named year Gregory XV. appointed a Vicar-Apostolic.

During the reign of James II. in 1688 Pope Innocent XI. created four districts for England and Wales. This arrangement lasted for the long period of two years over a century and a half. Pope Gregory XVI. on July 3, 1840, increased the districts to eight.

The Catholics of England had long desired to be ruled by bishops possessing English titles, and to this end the Catholic Committee for some time directed their attention.

But it has been remarked by a great prelate who was intimately connected with the movement which resulted in the re-establishment of the hierarchy that the "Holy See never acts or decides unless it sees the whole of a question, and sees clear throughout; whenever there is protracted delay, it is because the subject has not come before it in a form complete and adequate".[1]

The commencement of the movement which led to the re-establishment of the hierarchy may be dated from the year 1838, and it "was originated by Dr. Rock, chaplain to John, Earl of Shrewsbury, at Alton Towers. A petition to Pius IX. was adopted, and a committee of the elder clergy was chosen to draw it up and forward it to Rome. There the matter ended for a time; but in 1843 a little club of priests, called the Adelphi, formed themselves into a brotherhood for the restoration of the hierarchy. In 1845 Bishop Griffiths openly proposed a scheme for a petition to the Holy See for the restoration of the hierarchy, in so far as changing the Vicars-Apostolic into titular Bishops of England. Then other prelates seconded the proposition. Dr. Wiseman and Bishop Sharples were delegated to proceed to Rome to forward the petition."

For a time the process remained in abeyance; but in May, 1848, the bishops assembled in London, and Bishop Ullathorne

---

[1] The late Archbishop of Cabasa, better known as Dr. Ullathorne, first Bishop of Birmingham, author of *The History of the Restoration of the Catholic Hierarchy in England*.

was requested at once to proceed to Rome in furtherance of the scheme. "The Pope appointed a special congregation of seven cardinals to discuss and settle the question of the English hierarchy. Bishop Ullathorne presented a memorial to the Holy Father, in which were shown the disadvantages under which the English prelates and the Church in England then labored. The Holy Father assured the Bishop of his affection for the English Vicars and their clergy, and expressed his desire to concede their request. Owing to the absence of the Holy Father from Rome, in consequence of the action of the revolutionaries of 1848, the movement was necessarily retarded; but on September 29, 1850, 'the very flourishing kingdom of England was to be one single ecclesiastical province, with one Archbishop and twelve Suffragans'."[1]

Many writers have dealt with this question, but few have done so in the spirit of fair-mindedness equal to that of a Protestant ecclesiastic whose account we here summarise: "Up to 1850 the Roman Catholics of England had been ruled by bishops *in partibus infidelium*. At that time there were eight districts or vicariates. The Pope, in making the announcement, stated that in his judgment he felt that the circumstances of the times had rendered the government of the Catholics of England by vicars-apostolic no longer necessary, and he appointed one archbishop and twelve bishops. Dr. Wiseman was raised to the rank of cardinal." "Lord John Russell," says our authority, "was deeply offended at the conduct of the Tractarians who had taken exception to his episcopal appointments."[2] Herein then lay, according to this Protestant historian, one of the reasons for the agitation which a great English statesman thought fit to promote against this most harmless movement.

Then was issued by Lord John Russell the famous letter to the Bishop of Durham, an epistle better known as the "Durham Letter". In it Lord John considered "the late aggression of the Pope upon our Protestantism as insolent and insidious". The writer professed his desire to "promote to the utmost of his power" the claims of the Roman Catholics to all civil rights! But the head and front of the offending did not apparently consist so

---

[1] The portions quoted above of this account bearing quotation marks are extracted from Ramsay's *Life of Bishop Grant*, p. 68.

[2] Canon Molesworth's *History of the Church of England from 1660*.

much in Papal aggression as did the development of Catholic teaching in Protestant churches. The Tractarian movement was in full swing, Ritualism was at work, Catholic churches were springing up, the number of priests had increased of late. Lord John Russell made no secret of his real fears, for at the end of his letter he made these admissions: "There is a danger, however, which alarms me much more than any aggressions of a foreign sovereign. The clergymen of our Church who have signed the Thirty-nine Articles and acknowledged in explicit terms the Queen's supremacy have been the most forward in leading their flocks step by step to the very verge of the precipice." Lord John further complained that the Anglican clergy claimed infallibility for their Church; there was "the superstitious use of the sign of the cross, the muttering of the liturgy so as to disguise the language in which it is written, the recommendation of auricular confession and the administration of penance and absolution —all these things are pointed out by clergymen of the Church of England as worthy of adoption, and are now openly reprehended by the Bishop of London in his charge to the clergy of the diocese".

At this time the attitude of Cardinal Wiseman was most dignified, and this will be best shown by again quoting our Protestant authority.

"Scarcely was the ink dry before Lord John Russell received from Cardinal Wiseman an explanation which must have satisfied him of the injustice of many of the charges against the Pope that it contained, and must have caused him to regret having launched these elements of bitterness among a highly excited population without previous consultation with his colleagues, and at a moment when it was likely to cause a serious breach of the peace. For it was sent out at a time when the discovery of the Gunpowder Plot was about to be commemorated, and effigies of Guy Fawkes were committed to the flames, in memory of the happy escape of James I. and his Parliament. On this occasion the Pope and his cardinals figured in the place of Fawkes and were consumed amidst rioting, bonfires, squibs, and tar-barrels. Fortunately no serious mischief was done."

There is no doubt that the anti-"aggressionist" would have beat a retreat without a sacrifice of political dignity had such a course been possible. A comic journal caricatured him in the character of a little boy who, having chalked "No Popery" on the walls, was in the act of running away, afraid of the consequences of his action.

Be that as it may, the letter was soon followed up by action. The Parliament of 1851 was opened on 4th February, and three days later Lord John Russell introduced his "Ecclesiastical Titles Bill".

On 4th July the bill reached its final stage, and was sent to the Lords. There, after a debate of two nights, it went through Committee and was sent back to the Commons substantially as it had left. Soon after the "Royal Assent was given to the measure". In this progress through the House of Commons there was by no means unanimous assent. Mr. Gladstone, in opposing the bill, said : " It is hostile to the institutions of the country, more especially to its established religion, because it would teach us to rely on other support than that of the spiritual strength and vitality which alone can give it vigor ". But pass the bill did, yet it was a mere politico-religious fiasco, and by many thoughtful people was so regarded.[1]

The "Durham Letter" was undoubtedly calculated to raise a hostile feeling towards the Catholic body ; but, fortunately, there was no violence used. The hostility spent itself in sermons and newspaper articles. Happily for the Catholics, they had a tower of strength and an able defender in Dr. Newman, who, when the "Papal Aggression" fever was at its height, delivered his well-known lectures. In one of these discourses ("Fable the Basis of the Protestant View") the learned lecturer remarked : " The hatred and jealousy entertained by the population towards the Catholic Faith, and the scorn and pity which are felt at its adherents, have not passed away, have not been mitigated. . . . How is it that the feeling against Catholicism has remained substantially what it was in the days of Charles II. or George III. ? "

We shall best sum up the results of this agitation by quoting

---

[1] "While these things were being transacted in Parliament and in the country, Cardinal Wiseman was treating the demonstrations, of which he was the chief object, with tranquil regard. As already remarked, he had written to Lord John Russell a sensible letter, in which he pointed out that the substitution of bishops for vicars-apostolic, and the changes made in the arrangements of the dioceses were purely ecclesiastical arrangements, which might not have caused alarm. Lord John Russell probably repented of the precipitation with which he had acted, but it was too late for him to withdraw from the position he had taken up."—Molesworth's *History of the Church of England from* 1660.

the terse language of a modern writer of history, who, writing of the " Aggression," observes : " Nothing came of the Papal Bull. The Archbishop of Canterbury and the Bishop of London retained their places. Cardinal Wiseman remained only a prelate of the Roman Catholics. On the other hand, the ' Ecclesiastical Titles Act' was never put in force. Nobody troubled about it. Many years after, in 1871, it was quietly repealed. It died in such obscurity that the outer public hardly knew whether it was above ground or below." [1]

---

[1] M'Carthy's *History of Our Own Times*, vol. ii.

At the time of the re-establishment of the hierarchy various were the views held as to the expediency or inexpediency of the action of Pius IX. and the English bishops. Some Catholics were alarmed at the step taken, considering it premature. That the Holy See and the bishops were the best judges is now generally recognised ; and it is admitted that their action gave a great impetus to the expansion of the Church in England and Wales.

But lest any doubt should exist on this, we will quote the words of the present Holy Father, Leo XIII., who, thirty-one years after the hierarchy had become an accomplished fact, wrote in the constitution *Romanos Pontifices* :—

" That the Roman Pontiffs who have gone before us have cherished a fatherly love for the illustrious English nation we know from the records of history and from the solid proofs enumerated by Pius IX., of happy memory, in his bull *Universalis Ecclesiæ*, of September 29, 1850. As that bull restored the Episcopal hierarchy in England, he thereby crowned the measure of benefits conferred by the Holy See on that nation. For by this restoration of diocesan government that portion of Christ's fold already called to the wedding feast of the Lamb, and become a member of His mystic body, acquired a fuller and more stable possession of the truth and order through the rule and government of their bishops. . . . The subsequent events wonderfully corresponded to this wise design of [Pius IX.] ; for several provincial councils were celebrated which passed salutary laws for the regulation of diocesan matters; the Catholic faith received thereby daily increase, and many persons distinguished for their rank and learning returned to the unity of the Church. The clergy were much increased in number; as was increased the number of religious houses, not only of those belonging to the regular orders, but of those belonging to more recent institutes, and which rendered great services to religion and the State by educating the young and practising works of beneficence. Many pious lay sodalities were founded, new missions were established, and a great number of churches arose, splendid specimens of architecture and magnificently decorated. Then numerous asylums were created for orphans, together with seminaries, colleges and schools, in which a multitude of young children are trained to piety and the knowledge of letters."—O'Reilly's *Life of Leo XIII.*, p. 418.

CHAPTER XVI.

FATHER IGNATIUS SPENCER.

To present a passing sketch of the men of eminence and learning who during the past half-century have joined the Church would be a task voluminous in character, and more befitting a special record than the brief sketches here given. There are some, however, who, on account of their individuality or position, demand in an essay like this something more than a mere reference. It was in 1830 that the Hon. and Rev. George Spencer was converted to the Catholic Faith. The event was an extraordinary one, and at that time unique. That a scion of a noble house, a Church of England clergyman, a man of culture and affluence should abjure the religion of his fathers and join the communion of a hitherto despised sect was indeed a matter of surprise. Still greater was the wonderment when Mr. Spencer took on himself a life of self-denial by embracing the priesthood. It seemed like a Divine dispensation that this man of promise, possessed of all the qualities and qualifications that go to adorn society, should become an illustrious ornament of the Church. Yet so it was ordained. To read the life of Father Ignatius, as told by one of his brethren,[1] is like reading chapters from the lives of the saints. In comparison to the sacrifices he made there was no modern parallel. In his records of youth he frequently accused himself of cowardice, but to fully acquaint ourselves of his courageous action we must examine what is told of the noble Christians of Rome in the infancy of the Church.[2] True, there was no actual persecution to undergo, but there was the world to combat, a cutting asunder the bonds of friendship, the foregoing of pleasure, promotion, worldly honor: all this and much more was discarded in order that he might take up his cross and follow Christ. To the reader the question may present itself, who and what was this Father Ignatius, the hard-working priest, the missioner, the fervent religious? We give his biographer's estimate.

"He was a Cambridge first class man, and must therefore

---

[1] *Life of Father Ignatius Spencer*, by Fr. Pius. Dublin: Duffy, 1866.
[2] See the late Cardinal Wiseman's beautiful story *Fabiola*.

have been a good mathematical and classical scholar. He spoke Italian and French almost without fault, and conversed very well in German. He was well read in the English Protestant divines, and knew Catholic theology with accuracy, and to an extent which his academical course would not lead us to expect. It may be said that his youth and manhood were spent over the pages of the best English writers and in the company often of the best living authors. Althorp and Spencer House were famous for their literary coteries, and the son of an earl who patronised men of talent, and gave unmistakable proofs of great talent himself, was not one to let such opportunities pass without profit." Not content with the rigors of the secular order, this man of God desired for himself still further mortification, and he became a member of the Passionist Order. What this involves we will relate in his biographer's words: "The idea of a Passionist's work will lead us to expect what his discipline must be. The spirit of a Passionist is a spirit of atonement; he says with St. Paul: 'I rejoice in my sufferings, and fill up those things that are wanting of the sufferings of Christ, in my flesh for His body, which is the Church'. For this cause the interior life of a Passionist is austere. He has to rise shortly after midnight from a bed of straw to chant matins and lauds, and spend some time in meditation. He has two hours' more meditation during the day, and altogether about five hours of choir-work in the twenty-four. He fasts and abstains from flesh meat three days in the week all the year round, besides Lent and Advent. He is clad in a coarse black garment; wears sandals instead of shoes; and practises other acts of penance of minor importance."

Just as other pious servants of God in many instances devoted their lives to certain objects, either in the propagation of particular devotions or the exercise of charity, so Father Spencer had an object. It was in 1838 he began the great work to which twenty-six years of his life were devoted—the moving of the Catholics everywhere for the conversion of England. To such as desire to acquaint themselves with the earnestness and continuity of his work in this cause, we would recommend a perusal of the account to be found in his biography; suffice it here to remark that "he travelled through England, Ireland, Scotland, and even Italy, Germany, and France, exhorting the people to their own sanctification, and forming themselves as it were into a sacred army, to pour forth prayers for the conversion of England". Between June, 1858, and September, 1864, Father Spencer gave no fewer than 245 missions. His end came with suddenness. It is not for us to mar the words of truth and eloquence which on the occasion of Father Spencer's obsequies fell from the lips of the late Archbishop of Cabasa. The words are these, and with them we bring to a conclusion this summary of Father Spencer's life : " How beautiful, how sublime, was his departure. Father Ignatius had often wished and prayed that, like his Divine Lord, like St. Francis Xavier, and like his dear friend and master in the spiritual life, Father Dominic, he might die at his post, yet deserted and alone. God granted him that prayer. He had just closed one mission, and was proceeding to another; he turned aside on his way to converse with a dear friend and godson; he was seen ten minutes before conversing with children. Was he only inquiring his way, or did he utter the last words of his earthly mission to those young hearts? And here alone, unseen but of God and His angels, he fell down, and that heart which had beaten so long for the love and conversion of England stopped in his bosom."

CHAPTER XVII.

THE CONVENT QUESTION.

EARLY in 1854 the Catholics of England were much agitated by the action of a body of people calling themselves the "Anti-Convent Committee". This committee was fortunate or otherwise in securing a parliamentary champion in the person of a Mr. Chambers. The object they had in view was sufficiently explained by the title which they adopted. The Catholic body lost no time in showing that any such measure as that contemplated would meet with strong opposition from them, and meetings were held in various parts of the country to protest against the intended outrage on their religion. This was followed up by an address issued in March, 1854, by the Catholics of Great Britain to their Protestant fellow-countrymen. The 28th of March was the day appointed for Mr. Chambers to name his committee on conventual and monastic institutions. In the debate which subsequently took place Lord John Russell said it was worth while for the House to answer whether it would insist on appointing this committee. When he had thought that the Roman Catholics were encroaching, he had interfered, at the hazard of their displeasure, but he did not see what was to be gained by this inquiry, not believing the cock-and-bull stories that had been told in supporting it. Mr. Bowyer moved that the order for the appointment of a committee be discharged, and this was carried by a majority of 57. In May following the adjourned debate was proceeded with. Mr. John Bright, in the course of an able speech in opposition to the Bill, said that there were in the United Kingdom 6,000,000 of people, taking every man, woman, and child, who supported the opposition to the proposal for a committee, which the minority in that House maintained. That minority was acting in harmony not with a majority only, but with the unanimous body of the Roman Catholic population, and they had a right to make use of all the forms of the House to prevent the members of another faith from insulting the faith to which they (the Catholics) belonged. Lord John Russell answered that the passing of such a motion would tend to embitter the feelings between Roman Catholics and Protestants. Lord E. Howard disclaimed all desire to resort to factious opposition, but he thought hon. members were justified in resorting to every means in their power to defeat an attack upon them. The general feeling of the House was against the motion, and Mr. Chambers ultimately withdrew it. The conclusion of this fiasco is thus summed up : " The House divided—Ayes being 100 ; noes, 1 ; majority, 99 ".

Some years subsequently the Convent question was again revived by two eccentric members of Parliament, but, to the credit and good sense of the British Parliament, their efforts were abortive. During the past two Parliaments nothing has been said on the question, and the agitation connected with the ideas and efforts of a few persons on this particular question may now be looked upon as a thing of the past.

CHAPTER XVIII.

THE VATICAN DECREES.

IN November, 1874, considerable sensation was caused in the religious and literary circles of England through the publication by Mr. Gladstone of a pamphlet entitled " The Vatican Decrees in their Bearing on Civil Allegiance ". This was a revival in a mild and scholarly manner of the views held and statements made by prominent English Protestants in the early part of the present century, and later on when the hierarchy was re-established in England. The chief contention of the pamphlet was that the spiritual jurisdiction of the Pope was at times so interpreted as to bear directly on the civil allegiance of the subject to the constitution : in other words, that the spiritual power of the Pope could at times be directed so as to be exercised on matters purely political. For many years there had been no expression of opinion from any prominent politician which called forth excitement equal to that of the "Vatican Decrees" pamphlet.[1] The only parallel was that of the " Durham Letter," published nearly a quarter of a century before.

Mr. Gladstone then issued a second pamphlet in reply to his critics. In this publication he took occasion to remark: " I cannot but say that the immediate purpose of my appeal has been attained in so far that the loyalty of our Roman Catholic fellow-subjects in the mass remains untainted and secure ".[2]

This was a generous admission, and it conceded nearly all that the English Catholics sought for, and, indeed, was the aim of their remonstrances. The pamphlet was also remarkable for another expression of opinion, and it is here quoted as being the deliberate expression of a member of the Church of England, and one who may be regarded as a representative of English culture in the nineteenth century. Criticising Dr. Newman's "Letter to the Duke of Norfolk," Mr. Gladstone wrote of his opponent: "In my opinion his [Newman's] secession from the Church of England has never yet been estimated among us at anything like the full amount of its calamitous importance. It has been said that the world does not know its greatest men, neither, I will add, is it aware of the power and weight carried by the words and by the acts of those among its greatest men whom it does not know. The ecclesiastical historian will perhaps judge that this secession was a much greater event than even the partial secession of John Wesley, the only case of personal loss suffered by the Church of England since the Reformation which can be compared to it in magnitude."

---

[1] It brought forth no fewer than twenty-one pamphlets, besides numerous articles in the reviews. In the list of those who combated Mr. Gladstone's conclusions were Dr. Newman (" Letter to the Duke of Norfolk "), Dr. Manning, Dr. Clifford, Dr. Vaughan, Mgr. Capel, Canon Oakely, Mgr. Nardi (who published a reply in Italian), and several distinguished laymen.

[2] *Vaticanism*, Feb., 1875, p. 14.

CHAPTER XIX.

THE REUNION OF CHRISTENDOM.

WITH the progress of the present century has been witnessed a steady vanishing of the anti-Catholic spirit which was so much identified with the history of the Church during the first half of the present century. Opinions which obtained forty years ago are no longer held. The itinerant lecturer is now almost an institution of the past, and for some years we have been free from the riotous proceedings created by anti-Catholic lecturers. This is no doubt due to the spread of education, and the acquirement on a more extended scale of historical truth.

A quarter of a century ago the spirit of tolerance had so far progressed that there was a movement on foot for "The Reunion of Christendom," on the part of some well-meaning Protestant ecclesiastics. In other words, it was thought that the time had arrived when the Catholic Church could, in England at least, be levelled down to suit the whims of men who, however well-meaning in some respects, were lamentably deficient in judgment. With the Reunion of Christendom as interpreted by those outside the Church we have nothing to do, but the publication of the project called forth other expressions which come within the scope of our inquiry on the position of the Church in England at that period.

A distinguished Anglican[1] published in the year 1866, on the Reunion of Christendom, a criticism. To the Catholics that publication is of great interest, inasmuch as it may be considered as expressing the opinions generally held by the Church of England party at that period.

"Considering," said Dean Stanley, "what the no-Popery feeling has been in England; considering its intensity, its bitterness, its effects on the dismemberment of households and nations and in driving Protestants by reaction into the Church of Rome; considering the violence in which some of the best of our divines have indulged themselves in speaking of Roman Catholics to a degree far below the calm and measured language employed by our men of letters and our statesmen; considering all this, it seems to me a matter of sincere congratulation, not only that a book has been written (from whatever motive) speaking temperately of the Roman Catholic opinions which we condemn, but that the book has not excited any strong remonstrance on this point from any but the extremest partisans of the opposite school."

---

[1] Essays on *Church and State* by Dean Stanley. London: John Murray, 1870.

Dean Stanley's work is interesting from another point of view. It deals with the well-known "Tract Ninety" after the lapse of a quarter of a century.

"If ever there was a theological treatise under a ban it was 'Tract Ninety'. And now (1866) it is republished, virtually in the 'Eirenicon,' actually in the pamphlet which may be called a postscript to the 'Eirenicon'. Not a word of remonstrance. The heads of houses are silent. The bishops are silent. The leading journals even approve it, and consider the former outcry as 'ludicrously exaggerated and one-sided'."

Meanwhile the Church was steadily progressing. Alarmed at that progress, the "Scottish Reformation Society" published in 1867 something in the nature of an intended antidote. This took the form of a "map and table, showing the number and distribution of Roman Catholic establishments in England, Scotland, and Wales from 1838 to 1867". This was "drawn up and collected from Parliamentary and other official documents". The list stated that in England and Wales there were, in 1838, 423 chapels, and 1867, 926, showing an increase of 503. For Wales, between the years named, increase of chapels and stations was put as 10. This statement did not represent the actual increase, as will be seen from a comparison of these figures with those given in the official records of Catholic progress. To the society in question, however, it represented a most unsatisfactory state of things.

CHAPTER XX.

TWENTY-ONE YEARS' PROGRESS IN CATHOLIC EDUCATION.

THE statistics as to Catholic Elementary Education in England and Wales from 1870 to 1890 are as follow:—

Years.	No. of Schools.	Accommodation provided for.	Present at Inspection.	Government Grant.	Voluntary Subscription.	Voluntary Subscriptions for Twenty-one Years.	
				£	£		£
1870	350	101,556	83,017	31,665	22,387	1870-74	155,304
1874	567	...	119,582	54,330	40,025	1875-79	261,100
1879	737	242,403	159,576	102,625	54,428	1880-84	267,030
1884	828	284,514	200,158	137,702	57,672	1885-89	323,924
1889	920	334,032	221,446	164,412	67,480	1890	70,912
1890	946	341,953	223,645	167,736	70,912		
						Total, £1,078,270	

From the above tabulated statements, it will be seen that in twenty-one years the number of schools has been more than doubled, the accommodation more than trebled, the attendance at inspection has increased threefold. Voluntary subscriptions have increased over threefold, and more than a million of money has been subscribed by the Catholic body for the furtherance of education. In considering these statistics, it must also be borne in mind that in 1872 the time expired in which building grants and annual grants might be obtained for new voluntary schools. But in spite of this drawback the number of schools went on increasing.

Section 98 of the Elementary Education Act contained a sub-section for the refusal of grants to schools objected to by the Government for School Boards on the ground of "No deficiency of accommodation in the district".

In May, 1886, the Catholic Poor School Committee held its annual meeting, and in view of the recently appointed Royal Commission on Education, of which Cardinal Manning was a member, some interesting statistics were published in the report. From that report we quote the following: "The year's grant from the Parliamentary fund in 1852 was £7559 for the year ending 31st March, 1890, that is, before the Act came into operation it had risen to £37,283—since that Act it has by successive annual advances increased to the amount of last year, which was £185,756. The departments of schools in Great Britain receiving the annual grant in 1870 were 825, in 1885 they were 1695. The children in average attendance at the inspected Catholic schools in Great Britain before the Act of 1870 were 77,333; they had risen in 1885 to 208,447. Catholic teachers in primary schools in 1852 numbered 30; before the Act of 1870 the number given for inspected schools was 707, together with 82 assistant teachers. The teachers given in the returns for 1885 in inspected schools are 2317, together with 979 assistant teachers."

As instances of what may be termed specific progress as distinguished from general progress, the following particulars will doubtless prove of great interest, as showing the progress of Catholic education in given localities:—

At the annual meeting of the Westminster Diocesan Fund, held in 1888, the Cardinal-Archbishop of Westminster gave some interesting statistics as to the progress of education in the archdiocese. In 1866, which was the date of the first public meeting, there were in the diocese of Westminster 11,112 children in average attendance ; and at the day of inspection there were 11,145. In the inspector's report there was represented an average attendance of 19,532 ; and on the day of examination there were present 20,796. In the North Hyde School, in 1866, there were 70 boys, and that number had increased to 700. For the year (1888) there was an increase in the school books of 1600, and the schools had increased from 188 to 200. To sum up, there were 200 parochial schools, with 23,000 on the books, in 10 Poor Law schools 1600; in 3 industrial schools 467, in 1 reformatory school 167, in 7 orphanages 707 children ; making 26,227 as against the 11,000 with which they began 22 years previous.

In the diocese of Liverpool there were, in 1875, 48,455 children on the rolls, and in 1889 62,887 ; showing an increase of 14,432 children receiving Catholic education.[1] In the diocese of Birmingham there were in 1881 387 teachers, and in 1890 519 ; showing an increase of 132. In the same diocese in 1890 12,783 Catholic children were examined in religious knowledge, and 4019 non-Catholics. In one of the Birmingham schools over fifty per cent. of the children examined in religious knowledge were Protestants. At Banbury, in that diocese, the proportion of children stood—Catholic 139, non-Catholic 250 ; thereby exhibiting a preponderance of Protestant children of nearly 2 to 1. On the books of the 164 schools in the diocese there were 14,605 Catholic children and 6831 non-Catholic. These figures, strange as they may appear, bear out the remarks of the Government inspector of 1850 as to the preference frequently shown by Protestant parents for Catholic schools. The religious inspector for the diocese of Leeds gives the following statistics: In 1886 there were 3801 children on the register, 2352 in average attendance, and 2354 present at inspection. In 1890 the numbers were on the register 3500, average attendance 2653, present at inspection 2823.

In the diocese of Southwark in 1890 there were 2382 non-Catholic children attending Catholic schools, viz., London district, 783 ; Surrey country district, 288 ; Kent country district, 488 ; county of Sussex, 832.

In the report of the diocesan inspector for the archdiocese of

---

[1] Father Morris, article in *The Month*, March, 1891.

Westminster the percentage of passes for the year ending 31st August, 1889, stood:—

Catholic Schools	90·07
Board Schools	90·65
Wesleyan Schools	88·77
British Schools	88·62
Church of England Schools	87·83

The educational statistics for the diocese of Clifton exhibit the following during five years: In 1886 there were on the register 3081 children; average attendance, 2352; present at examination, 2354. The figures for 1890 were 3500, 2653 and 2823 respectively.

CHAPTER XXI.

THE ATTITUDE OF THE CHURCH ON EDUCATION. WHAT OF THE FUTURE?[1]

FOR twenty years the Catholics of this country have maintained a severe struggle in the all-important matter of elementary education, and out of that struggle they have emerged triumphant. And how has all this been accomplished? It has been accomplished by the ever-watchful care of the bishops and priests; by the noble efforts of the Poor School Committee; by the heads of training colleges and those in authority over teachers; by the charitable offices exercised by sisterhoods. And this work has been brought about too by the contributions of the rich and the pence of the poor, and lastly, though not in any sense of disparagement, by the skill and devotion to duty which our school teachers have brought to bear in their duties. And this skill and devotion to duty have been eminently characteristic of this deserving though underpaid class—a class whose exertions call for the

---

[1] "We have more than once said we strongly approve of the voluntary schools. ... We desire their increase as much as possible, and that they may flourish in the number of scholars. For it is in and by these schools that the Catholic faith, our greatest and best inheritance, is preserved whole and entire. In these schools the liberty of parents is respected, and what is most needed in the prevailing licence of opinion and of action, it is by these schools that good citizens are brought up for the State, for there is no better citizen than the man who has believed and practised the Christian faith from childhood."—Letter of Leo XIII. to the Bishops of England on Religious Education, 27th Nov., 1885.

thankful appreciation of the Catholics of England and Wales. But what of the future? Shall we continue to maintain our status as an educating body? This is a grave question, for in education great changes have been brought about. We have traced the history of education concerning the Catholic body from the beginning of the present century. We have seen how—unaided, weak, and with straitened circumstances—the Church struggled on up to the year 1870, increasing her efforts year by year. We have witnessed the efforts put forth during the past twenty years. What was done before the year 1870 was of a spontaneous or voluntary character assisted by the State. But in 1870 the State endeavoured to grasp the subject and sought to carry out another system. That system has had a trial of twenty years, but the education problem is not yet solved. It would scarcely be just to minimise the difficulties that have been in the way. There is no question that taxes to the utmost in a greater degree the wisdom of our statesmen than this great question. No question has farther-reaching effects. It enters into the hearths and homes of the people and concerns domestic existence. In 1886 a Royal Commission was appointed to inquire into the working of the Act of 1870, and the voluminous reports issued by that Commission will show how intricate is the question.

But to return to the query, What of the future? As we write the Legislature has announced that another education era is about to commence. Of this it is premature to speak further than that it will create another new condition. It will revolutionise the system which has hitherto obtained. The child will still more become a creature of the State, the parent will surrender his child yet more to State control. We do not argue that free education or assisted education, or what term soever it may be known by in the remission of school fees, will not be a relief and a financial boon to the poor people of this country, both Catholic and Protestant. But will the surrender be worth the price paid? Will the child by reason of this additional lien be considered more as a unit of the State? Into these questions we shall not profess to enter—to do so would be at present out of place. But of one thing we are certain, and it is, that if under struggling and adverse circumstances the Catholic body has done so much, that body will, if needs be, do still more. Every means will be exhausted to retain for the Catholic child the great blessing and the right of religious teaching day by day along with secular education.

The State may be, and no doubt is, justified in determining the quantity and the length of service to which children shall be subjected to supervision in so far as concerns secular knowledge.

But God has given to parents, over and above States and Governments, the charge of children, and any Government opposing or interfering with this principle is of necessity opposing laws both Divine and human. And in so far as relates to this country the Church, in defending religious teaching, is upholding a principle precious and dear to the English people—that of the right of a parent to decide as to the religion in which his or her child shall be instructed. The children of the last generation are the manhood and womanhood of this our own time. The precious heritage of the Catholic religion has been handed down to us by our parents, and but for the efforts of the Church, seconded by the laity, the Church could not have progressed in such a marvellous degree. The children of to-day are the hope and the future of the Church, and the blessings of religious teaching day by day must at all costs be preserved to them.

Whatever, then, may be done by the Legislature, there is certainty in this: That the Church, through her bishops, priests, and people, will strive in the future, as in the past, to imprint upon the youthful mind day by day the truths of the Catholic religion, thereby interpreting and carrying into effect the lessons to be learned from the words of wisdom of the Vicar of Christ on earth, viz., that "there is no better citizen than the man who has believed and practised the Christian religion from childhood".

CHAPTER XXII.

THE GENERAL PROGRESS OF CATHOLICISM IN ENGLAND AND WALES.

FROM this table it will be seen that, roughly speaking, the population of England and Wales has in forty years increased by 60 per cent. The figures we give show that the Church has made progress at the rate of 300 per cent. for priests, and 132 per cent. for churches. But it must also be considered that about 1847 commenced the large exodus from Ireland. That exodus distinctly represented an addition to the Catholic body. We may safely state that at the lowest computation half-a-million of Catholics

Churches.	1885.		1890.		Increase.	
	Priests.	Churches.	Priests.	Churches.	Priests.	Churches.
108	349	116	357	129	244	83
...	...	...	...	...	...	...
112	200	119	206	122	82	40
41	96	43	112	50	63	19
105	169	109	163	114	93	63
140	323	145	421	155	308	76
58	68	67	75	70	53	52
49	49	52	56	54	29	28
76	121	92	114	87	61	45
37	87	47	92	52	67	24
105	218	109	245	111	184	76
74	112	74	113	73	80	43
147	197	100	242	118	175	61
75	112	83	109	86	} 111	82
48	73	55	71	57		
...	82	58	102	57	102	57
C.	P.	C.	P.	C.		
1175	2256	1269	2478	1335	1652	749
80	1885		1890			

, 20th December, 1878.

land and Wales.

	Total.	Increase in each Decade.
1	17,927,609	...
ɔ	20,066,224	2,138,615
5	22,712,266	2,646,042
5	25,974,439	3,262,173
4	29,001,018	3,026,579
		11,073,409

have settled in England since the year 1847, and for these provision had to be made. Add to this number a computation of 60 per cent. increase, and we shall then be able to comprehend the increase of Catholics, especially in large towns. The statistics we present are of two kinds—first, an increase of priests and churches between 1851 and 1890; and, secondly, the *actual* position of the Church in regard to area and population. Analysing the first-named, it is observable that the greatest increase in the number of priests took place in the diocese of Liverpool, but in that diocese the increase of churches was not in proportion, as Salford, with an addition of 184 priests, shows an increase of exactly the same number of churches. But progress, whether in the matter of extra priests or churches, is equally a matter of gratulation. The Catholic Church, whether in England or elsewhere, is admirably adapted to meet the requirements of the people, and to an extent of which no other Church is capable. Where there is a thick cluster of the faithful, and difficulties in the way of building present themselves, the Church meets the requirements by an addition of priests. The same building may, and does frequently, serve for its five, six, seven, and even ten celebrations of Mass on the Sunday. This is a matter not generally understood by those outside the Church. Lancashire, which has a diocese within itself, and has also room for portion of another, contains many large towns where the people are grouped together. On the one hand, the increase of priests indicates a want of their services in given localities. Additional churches indicate needs for local wants, either by placing a church in a town or district where none has previously existed; or by increasing the number in a given locality, where, by reason of increase of Catholics, building has become a work of necessity. The next *apparent* increase is in that of the diocese of Westminster, which, like Liverpool, exhibits a great demand for priests.[1]

Southwark, had not Portsmouth been founded, would have been

---

[1] In a pastoral issued April, 1891, on the need for additional priests, the Cardinal-Archbishop of Westminster made use of the following words: "The old London vicariate of eight counties forty years ago had only 187 priests. The three dioceses sprung from it have now 702; and yet year by year we need more." It will be noted that the number quoted by His Eminence coincides almost exactly with those given in the tabulated statement; first in 1851 with the dioceses of Westminster and Southwark, and in 1890 for those dioceses with Portsmouth added.

second on the list. This diocese exhibits great recuperative power. Under ordinary circumstances the numbers for Southwark would have stood—priests, 244; churches, 175; showing in forty years an increase of 177 priests and 127 churches, and in the latter respect greatly in excess of any other diocese. In 1880 the churches were 252, and ten years later, notwithstanding the partition that had taken place, it had regained that number less ten only, the priests being fewer by 27. In a short time, therefore, Southwark will show the same numbers as ten years ago, allowing the foundation of a new diocese. Plymouth, Hexham, Shrewsbury, and Birmingham are next as showing an excellent increase of priests, and for churches Westminster, Liverpool, Salford, Hexham, and Southwark. Beverley, as a diocese, ceased in 1878. Had the name remained it would have shown excellent progress by an increase of 111 priests and 82 churches, and would have ranked in point of numbers next to Southwark. But Beverley's loss is shown in the gain of the two new dioceses of Leeds and Middlesborough.

Pursuing the analysis further, we have exactly three times the number of priests we had in 1851. To the number we then had are added exactly that total multiplied by two. The churches, as above stated, have been increased 130 per cent. In other words, where forty years ago the Catholics had one priest, there are now three; where they had three churches, we have now seven.

CHAPTER XXIII.

SPECIFIC AS DISTINGUISHED FROM GENERAL PROGRESS.

HAVING considered the question as to the progress of the Catholic Church in this country in one aspect, there are other phases to be dealt with. It has already been shown that progress real and effective has been made, but it is necessary that the statements made should be accepted, in a comparative sense, that is with a consideration of what the Church was a century or half-a-century ago, and what she is now. It is no detraction from what has already been advanced to assert that there are causes why the Church has not made even greater progress than that already recorded. What are the *apparent* causes which have tended in the direction of retarding an extension of the Church's power? First,

County.[1]	Population, 1891.[1]	No. of Churches and Chapels, 1890. A
Bedford	506,096	37
Berks	445,599	14
Bucks	185,938	13
Cambridge	20,659	2
Cheshire	236,324	13
Cornwall	484,326	29 including Bristol and Clifton
Cumberland	1,083,273	50
Derby	369,351	15
Devon	1,730,871	16 Country district
Dorset	550,442	36
Durham	805,070	45
Essex	66,098	4
Gloucester	264,969	7
Hampshire	413,755	18
Hereford	399,412	14
Herts	368,237	30
Huntingdon	2,441,164	90
Kent		
Lancashire	WALES.	
Leicester	50,079	1
Lincoln	57,031	1
London—	62,596	1
Middlesex, Essex	130,574	2
Herts	118,225	5
London—	117,950	3
Surrey, Kent	77,189	9
Sussex	687,147	20
Middlesex	49,204	1
Monmouth	58,003	1
Norfolk	89,125	3
Northampton	21,791	0

[1] Co[...] defines the number where Mass may be heard
A Th[...] ents, and domestic chapels have not been
on Sunda[...] of a complex character. For London we
counted; [...]nt and Sussex within the Diocese of South-
give the f[...]
wark, bes[...] or statistical purposes, however, and as a
Gre[...]
general o[...]

it can scarcely be denied that in many instances there has been a lavish expenditure in the erection of churches, on a scale more elaborate than has been requisite either from local circumstances or in connection with the general well-being of the Church or the needs of the Catholic body. Almost side by side are to be found the two extremes of wealth and poverty ; imposing churches with rich ornamentation on the one hand, and on the other meagreness and poverty. Is there no *via media* in this matter ? The progress of religion is not to be measured, we would submit, by the standard of Gothic architecture or by unnecessary display, but rather by the extension of the mandate that the poor should have the Gospel preached to them. Is this done to the extent it should or could be done ? We are forced to answer in the negative. It is notorious that in parts of England many thousands of pounds have been spent neither wisely nor well. It were surely better to have ten churches or chapels at a cost of a thousand pounds each than one costing £10,000. Moreover, the straining for elaborateness has other effects : it impoverishes the people for a number of years, and both people and clergy are continually laboring to wipe away heavy debts, and this alone is a barrier to progress.

How many of our churches and chapels are consecrated ? Few indeed, for the reason that they are still burthened with debt. So long as it can be said—and this can now be said—that there are within England alone a number of towns of considerable size where there is no Sunday Mass, so long will the Catholic body have reason to consider they have not attained to a full and satisfactory progress. England, and the fact must be admitted, is a Protestant country. The Anglican movement was one affecting the learned and the rich. What is desired is that it be extended to the middle classes, and the toilers. In the rural districts of England particularly the knowledge of Catholic doctrines is utterly unknown. We have missions, and happily, schools provided, but a *missionary spirit* is desirable, an extension of the principle which governs the regular clergy. In other words, the principle of the Catholic secular clergy living in communities and thus being in readiness to go into the highways and byeways and preach the Gospel and the truths of the Catholic religion. It is useless to wait for miracles to take place, remembering that God helps those who help themselves. We have around us abundant testimony to the work of Wesley. Yet Wesley had practically to found a new religion. To-day the towns and villages of England and

Wales are covered with temples bearing his name. Not that the express methods of Wesley should be copied by the Catholic Church; but there are ways and means of developing a principle. The English people are a susceptible people—they will listen to reason and argument.

To an unbelieving world the preaching of St. Dominic, St. Francis Assissi, and St. Ignatius Loyola may have appeared out of the ordinary. Yet these saints were as great pillars to the Catholic Church. St. Vincent of Paul, by his humility and unpretentious methods, founded an organisation as noble as any the Church possesses. Not that the beauty and form of the churches should for a moment be put aside as unworthy of consideration. On the contrary, where practicable, these are praiseworthy considerations, and are in full accord with the spirit of the Church. But the end will be defeated where the principle is carried out at the expense of, or to the detriment of, the general progress of religion. Churches and chapels are erected primarily, that they may afford to the people a place wherein to receive the consolations of religion, and other matters should be made subsidiary to the first and greatest consideration.

How wonderful to contemplate the sacrifices made by the leaders of the Anglican movement! They gave up position, station, future prospects—and for what? To accept the religion of a poor and hitherto proscribed class. Sixty years ago, when George Spencer embraced the Catholic religion, his action represented no ordinary event. That great man may be said to have been the proto-convert, the forerunner of what has long been known as the Tractarian movement. For men of learning to embrace Catholicism was looked upon as an act of supreme folly—like that of embracing the notions of Buddha or Mahomet.[1]

Yet it was done, and it must be admitted that the results of the action of these men of eminence are not commensurate with the expectations formed. The Church has successfully asserted her

---

[1] For more than a quarter of a century Father Spencer was earnestly engaged in the work of the conversion of England. On every possible occasion, when giving missions and retreats in every grade of society, he begged for prayers for that most laudable object. Considering this, it is a melancholy reflection that to-day the district traversed by Father Spencer in 1830, when proceeding from Northampton to Leicester, to make his submission to the Church, is almost in the same position with regard to Catholic population as it was sixty years ago.

dominion and power over intellect, position, and wealth ; and now to complete the conquest she needs the rank and file also. Surely there is room for the spreading among the English people of the solid truths of the Catholic religion, especially when we remember that within recent years there have been many in this country who have shown a willingness to accept as a guide to sanctity the claims of a new organisation whose system is based upon grotesque exhibitions and hysterical ranting. It is no argument to say that the masses of English people are indifferent about religion. That is the outcome of the various systems that have held good these three hundred years. But that condition *is* an argument for increased watchfulness and need for the expansion of Catholic teaching. Two fundamental articles of the Catholic Church have been observed in the past in Protestant England more than they are now observed. The passing of the measure in 1857 for facilitating Divorce has led to a vast increase in the number of divorces. Baptism is not considered a requisite. Both baptism and the Indissolubility of matrimony are Catholic dogmas which lie at the root of Christianity itself. Matrimony is that Sacrament upon which depends the domestic existence, and it is a guarantee of the cohesion of Christian society. But, we repeat, there would appear to be a loosening of the hold of the English people in these two requisite observances, hence the need for Catholic teaching thereon.

Again, with respect to our seminaries, we have a superabundance, paradoxical as the term may seem. In other words, we want less division, more centrality. We have in England, as is well known, several seminaries, and the question suggests itself, Does this multiplicity indicate want of organisation and a division of power? In the scholastic system such methods would be disastrous. More than one training college could not be maintained on account of the cost—not only the initial cost of building, but in maintenance and teaching staff. It will generally be conceded that the division of teaching power tends to a weakening of teaching power. Why so? Because professors of theology, like other professors, should have adequate emolument, otherwise their services can scarcely be expected. Again, it is manifestly impossible to have a division of intellect for each seminary. Why should the services of a distinguished professor of theology be exhausted upon half-a-dozen students (under the division system) when the same could be rendered to a hundred or more? The half-dozen may be filled to repletion, but that is no consolation to the ninety-four who go empty away. This division of teaching power, this want of massing together our ablest men and all the students, most certainly will have this tendency: that the clergy, for want of participation in the benefits of centrality, must necessarily be less proficient in intellectual acquirements. Or put in another form, with improved advantages they would be better equipped. The cost of training is not the least consideration, as under the system now in vogue the expense must be heavy, and the adoption of two or three centres would tend to a considerable reduction in the cost of the training of our priesthood. This, again, would have its effect on supply. Prosaic as the consideration may be, it is unquestionable that the supply and demand are considerably affected by pecuniary aspects.

An examination of the table (p. 100A) will demonstrate the fact that the country districts of England and Wales are sparsely provided for in the matter of churches. After deducting from the totals the figures for the cities and larger towns, such as London, Liverpool, Manchester, Birmingham, Leeds, Preston, Wolverhampton, &c., it will be apparent that few churches and chapels are allocated for other portions of the counties.

Turning to Wales, we find that, with the exception of some seaside resorts in the north, and the county of Glamorgan in the south, to the Catholic Church the Principality is almost a *terra incognita*. There are five counties with only one church each, and one county has not a single church, chapel, or station. Of the twenty churches and chapels in Glamorgan, Cardiff claims five. This unsatisfactory state of things may be ascribed chiefly to the passionate attachment of the Welsh people to their language, and little progress can be looked for in Wales until there are Welsh-speaking priests, and Catholic prayer-books printed in the vernacular. The majority of the Welsh people, as is well known, are Dissenters, and their books of devotion are printed in the language of the people. Frequently, too, there are bi-lingual services, and no effort has been spared by the Dissenting bodies to consider the prejudices of the people, and particularly that of the maintenance of the Welsh language.

For the Church to make progress in Wales, we conclude that the first consideration must of necessity consist in paying due regard to the national customs of the people, in which the preservation of the language shall prominently take part.

CHAPTER XXIV.

RECENT EVENTS—1870-1890.

DURING the past twenty-one years there have been many occurrences of interest to the Catholic body, and we give a summary thereof to bring down our review to the present time. Of the year 1870 it is interesting to note that there were present at the Œcumenical Council, " any time between 8th December, 1869, and 8th July, 1870, the Archbishop of Westminster and ten bishops," representing the English hierarchy. Whilst progress has been made at home, the Catholic body have not been unmindful of the duty of spreading the faith in foreign parts by sending out missionaries. For this excellent object St. Joseph's Foreign Missionary Society at Mill-Hill was commenced in 1863. The work was inaugurated in 1866 with one student and one servant. In April, 1868, a public meeting was held in St. James's Hall. Archbishop Manning presided, and there were eight bishops present. In June, 1869, the first stone of the present college was laid. The first stone of the Memorial Church was laid, St. Joseph's Day, 1871, and was opened two years later on the same feast.

The good work done by the college is so widely known that comment would be superfluous.

In March, 1875, the Archbishop of Westminster was raised to the purple. The election of Dr. Manning to the cardinalate was without doubt the first case in which at Englishman and a convert had attained that high rank.

In 1879 great was the joy of the English Catholics when in the month of April it became known that the Holy Father had notified his intention to raise the venerable John Henry Newman, priest of the Oratory of St. Philip Neri, to the rank of a Prince of the Church. Protestants as well as Catholics seemed joyful at the news, and when the distinguished churchman started on his long journey to the Eternal City his progress from place to place was watched with great solicitude. Dr. Newman set out for Rome April 16, 1879, and arrived in the Eternal City on the 24th. He received from the Holy Father a most cordial welcome. The formal announcement of his creation as Cardinal Deacon was conveyed to him on May 12 at the Palazzo della Pigna, where a brilliant throng of English and American Catholics and of high dignitaries, lay and ecclesiastical, surrounded him.[1]

In 1880 was passed a measure which was certainly one of "relief" to the Catholics. We allude to the passing of the "Burial Laws Amendment Act" (44 Vic. cap. 41). Prior to the passing of this Act, as is well known, the majority of burial places were under the control of the Church of England. No Catholic priest could officiate at the last solemn rites, a function of the utmost importance, and a corporal work of mercy, not to speak of the religious aspect. Under this system it was the custom for Catholics to have the burial service read in the house of the deceased person, after which the body was conveyed to the churchyard, the Church of England service being read at the interment. This anomaly obtained until the year 1880, when happily, by the efforts of liberal-minded men, it was relegated to the past.

On September 26, 1886, was celebrated the centenary of St. George's Cathedral, Southwark. Cardinal Manning, in a sermon preached on that occasion, gave a sketch of the position of Catholics during the preceding century, that is, from 1786. From it we summarise the following, inasmuch as it may be looked upon as a review of the condition of the Church within the metropolis for one hundred years : " One hundred years ago a humble and zealous priest for £20 hired a room, and in that room he offered the Holy Sacrifice of the Mass. Afterwards a chapel—for under the penal laws no one ventured to talk about a church—a chapel was built that would contain a thousand persons. Between 1830 and 1847 or 1848 this church was begun and was perfected. And on the day that this cathedral was opened there was an assemblage of Catholic pastors such as I believe England had not seen for three hundred years." Such was the condition of affairs one hundred years ago, and the contrast between that time and the present is striking in the extreme. But there is more than this. In his sermon the Cardinal further demonstrated that this progress was not confined to London, but applied with equal truth to other parts of the country. In the sermon from which we have already quoted His Eminence used these words : "I will give you an example of what I mean. The cathedral of Southwark was once the cathedral of the London Vicariate, and that London Vicariate has now three dioceses : Westminster,

---

[1] Dr. Barry's *Outline of the Life of Cardinal Newman* : Catholic Truth Society.

Southwark, and Portsmouth. There were, in the year 1850, 169 priests for what is now three dioceses. The priests of these dioceses are now over 600. In all the centuries before the hierarchy the priests were never multiplied as they have been since they have become the pastors of the flock. The Northern Vicariate of Lancashire, Yorkshire, Northumberland and North Cumberland at that time had 320 priests. The vicariate has now five dioceses, and it has 890 priests."

It has been already observed that much of the history of the Catholic Church is the history of persecution and of martyrdom. In January, 1887, took place an event which filled the English Catholics with joy, viz., the beatification of fifty-four English martyrs who suffered death between the years 1535 and 1583 under Henry VIII. and Elizabeth. From the official decree we learn that: "Until lately the cause of these martyrs had never been officially treated. Some time ago, in the year 1860, Cardinal Nicholas Wiseman, of illustrious memory, Archbishop of Westminster, and other Bishops of England, petitioned the Sovereign Pontiff, Pius IX., of sacred memory, to institute for the whole of England a festival in honor of all holy martyrs, that is to say, even of those *who, though not yet declared to be such, have in later times, for their defence of the Catholic religion, and especially for asserting the authority of the Apostolic See, fallen by the hands of wicked men and resisted unto blood.* But as, according to the prevailing practice of the congregation of Sacred Rites, a festival can be instituted in regard only to those servants of God to whom ecclesiastical honor (*cultus*) has been already given and rightly sanctioned by the Apostolic See, the said petition was not granted. Wherefore in these last years a new petition was presented to our Holy Father the Sovereign Pontiff, Leo XIII., by His Eminence Cardinal Henry Edward Manning, the present Archbishop of Westminster, and the other Bishops of England, together with the Ordinary Process which had been there completed, and other authentic documents in which were contained the proofs of martyrdom as to those who suffered from the year 1535 to 1583, and also the aforesaid concessions of the Roman Pontiffs in regard to those above-mentioned.

"By a wonderful dispensation of Providence, a full record of the troublous times and the names of the martyrs was preserved in a manner almost miraculous. Gregory XIII. . . . after he had caused the sufferings of the Christian martyrs to be painted in fresco by

Nicholas Circinani in the Church of St. Stephen on the Cœlian Hill, permitted also the martyrs of the Church in England, both of ancient and of more recent times, to be represented in like manner by the same artist in the English Church of the Most Holy Trinity in Rome, including those who, from the year 1535 to the year 1583, had died under King Henry VIII. and Queen Elizabeth for the Catholic faith and for the primacy of the Roman Pontiff. The representations of these martyrdoms painted in the said church remained with the knowledge and approbation of the Roman Pontiffs who succeeded Gregory XIII. for two centuries, until about the end of the last century they were destroyed by wicked men. But copies of them still remained, for in the year 1584, by privilege of the said Gregory XIII., they had been engraved at Rome on copper-plate with the title—' Sufferings of the Holy Martyrs who, in ancient and more recent times of persecution, have been put to death in England for Christ, and for professing the truth of the Catholic Faith '."

In 1887 there were two interesting occurrences. In the month of June was celebrated the Jubilee of the reign of Queen Victoria. In May the Holy Father apprised the Prime Minister of his desire to send a special mission of congratulation to the Court of St. James. This was followed up on 10th June by a letter from Leo XIII. to Queen Victoria, in which occurred these words: " For our part as chief of the Catholic Church, which counts so many faithful among the subjects of your Majesty, and knowing the full and entire liberty which, in your clear-seeing justice, you assure the exercise of their religion, we are unable to abstain from being represented at these rejoicings and from renewing to your Majesty the testimony of gratitude and high esteem which, at the time of our Nunciature at Brussels, we had the opportunity of personally expressing to you". This letter was entrusted to Monsignor Ruffo-Scilla, and in due course presented to her Majesty, together with appropriate presents. On the 18th July following this was acknowledged by the Queen, who in so doing assured the Holy Father of the " sincere friendship and unfeigned respect and esteem " which she entertained for his person and character.[1] A

---

[1] The celebration of this was first proposed by a Catholic peer—Lord Braye, in a letter to the *Times*, Sept. 2, 1885. It was not celebrated, however, till 1887, *i.e.*, the fifty-first year of Victoria. George III. kept his jubilee in the fiftieth year of his reign—1809.

few months later there was a further interchange of expressions of esteem. The sacerdotal jubilee of Leo XIII. was celebrated in the year 1888, and in anticipation of the event the Queen on 15th November, 1887, despatched a special mission to the Vatican to congratulate the Holy Father, and the mission bore as gifts from the Queen an ewer and basin. The Queen entrusted the gifts to the Duke of Norfolk as special envoy, and the letter and accompanying gifts were duly acknowledged by the Pope in writing on 3rd January, 1888.[1]

CHAPTER XXV.

CONCLUSION.

In bringing to a conclusion this brief review of the Church's history in this country during the past two hundred years, it is requisite that consideration be given to these questions: Has the Church made progress during that period, or has she been retrograde or stationary? Above all, has the Church progressed within our own time? Has there been loss on a scale detrimental or dangerous to her future? Has the loss (assuming there is loss, small or great) corresponded to her gain, or has the gain which has admittedly taken place been counterbalanced by the loss of numbers born within the fold of the Church, but who from indifferentism or other causes can no longer be considered Catholics? These questions are indeed of great moment to every Catholic who has at heart the well-being of the Church. In attempting to answer them there is great difficulty, especially when it is borne in mind that contrary opinions are held by Catholics who have given to this matter careful consideration. To those who may consider that the Church has not progressed as she should have done, or that the loss has been extensive, every consideration ought to be given, bearing in mind that their views are the result of anxiety for the Church's future. To the all-important question, Has the Church progressed within our own time? we are forced to the conclusion that an answer in the affirmative is a truthful reply,

---

[1] A full account of these proceedings was published by the Government, and presented as a Blue Book to both Houses of the Legislature.

and that the Church has progressed to a most gratifying degree. Is the alleged loss as extensive as some are inclined to state? Is it in a degree lesser or greater than that of any Protestant sect? No Catholic will minimise or attempt to make light the loss to the Church of a single soul. But no one will deny that there is loss of some kind, and this will continue to be a characteristic of the Catholic Church in common with all denominations. Whether that loss be great or small is a question that may fairly be left for the bishops and clergy to deal with, and there can be no doubt it will be dealt with just as have other pressing needs. There is one apparent loss, however, of which it would be desirable to take cognisance in connection with the subject of loss and gain. This loss consists in the emigration from England of great numbers of Catholics whose destination is chiefly that of the United States of America. For years this system of drainage has been going on, but few writers seem to have measured the loss to the Catholic body thereby sustained. That this draining process has taken place and does take place may be borne out by any priest stationed for a few years within the towns regarded as manufacturing centres. It is true that these emigrants still remain Catholics, and go to swell and increase the power and extend the Church in America or elsewhere, but it represents a direct loss to the Church in England. Between the gloomy views of the pessimists, and the exaggerations of the optimists, there are medium considerations and questions, and they are: Has the Church, all things considered, increased in numbers and position? Are her members socially in a better condition than at any other time within the past two hundred years? To these questions we unhesitatingly answer, Yes. From reliable statistics we have shown how priests and churches have increased, and that the Catholic body has been foremost in education work. As to the social status we know that the Catholic body is well represented in the highest grades of society, and that the Catholics are now members of the judicature, magistracy, and frequently leaders in local governing bodies. Why, therefore, shall we not in looking at these things be jubilant? Why not have reason for thankfulness at the position of the Church to-day compared with that of the gloomy past? At no time within the past three hundred years was the Church in a more flourishing condition than at the present day. Never were there more agencies for doing good. Within recent years sodalities have increased, convents have sprung up all over the country, asylums for the aged and infirm have been established. And what of the English people in their attitude to the Church? Has it not changed? Are not Catholics looked upon as friends and brethren rather than as aliens? On this let a great authority speak: "Since the year 1838, some thirty millions at least have been spent on Christian education. These are not the works of a people which have ceased to be Christian. Mutilated indeed its Christianity may be, and robbed of sacramental grace, yet there never was any time when the will of multitudes was more liberated from anti-Catholic superstitions."[1] These are indeed words of truth, and the proof is visible around us. If any proof were needed, there is one event that stands out in bold relief, conveying as it does in a marked manner this change. In the month of August, 1890, there lay in the Oratory Church at Birmingham the remains of John Henry Newman, Cardinal Deacon of the Holy Roman Church. The whole of England was profoundly moved at the news of Newman's death, and it was universally felt that a great man had passed away. Protestant England paid such a tribute as no Catholic had received within living memory, and the leading organ of the country ventured to assert that Newman's name would be canonised and enshrined in the hearts of the people of England.

To sum up the conclusions as to the Church's progress, and her actual position to-day, we submit: That the Church has progressed during the past fifty years; that that progress has been specific and visible in the large centres of population; that the extensive emigration of Catholics to other countries has tended to minimise that progress; that in the urban and rural districts of England and Wales the Church has made no progress but has remained stationary; that the cause of this is traceable (*a*) to the fact that many Catholic estates have changed hands during the past half-century; and (*b*) to the want of churches, a want which might have been obviated by a better disposition of sums of money lavished in many cases to a reckless and extravagant degree in places where the population has not warranted such outlay. We also affirm that it is most desirable that the people of England and Wales should have the opportunities afforded of learning the truths of the Catholic religion by the systematic erection of

---

[1] Cardinal Manning, *Dublin Review*, October, 1885.

churches, chapels, mission rooms, and schools in places where none now exist, to the end that this once Catholic country—" the Mother of Saints," as it has been called by the present visible Head of the Church —may have the means of receiving back the True Faith, and so hasten to accomplish in our midst the words of the Divine Founder of the Catholic Church: "There shall be One Fold, and One Shepherd".

FINIS.

www.ingramcontent.com/pod-product-compliance
Lightning Source LLC
Chambersburg PA
CBHW031400160426
43196CB00007B/833